ARCHER IN THE MARROW

Archer in the Marrow

THE APPLEWOOD CYCLES
of 1967–1987

PETER VIERECK

W · W · NORTON & COMPANY

New York · *London*

Published simultaneously in Canada by Penguin
Books Canada Ltd., 2801 John Street, Markham,
Ontario L3R 1B4.
Printed in the United States of America.

FIRST EDITION

The text of this book is composed in Garamond No. 3, with
display type set in Garamond Old Style. Composition and
manufacturing by the Maple-Vail Book Manufacturing Group.

Book design by Mary Cregan.

Library of Congress Cataloging in Publication Data
Viereck, Peter Robert Edwin, 1916–
Archer in the marrow.

I. Title.
PS3543.I325A88   1987   811'.54   83–22064

ISBN 0-393-02321-4

ISBN 0-393-30326-8 (PBK)

W. W. Norton & Company, Inc., 500 Fifth Avenue, New York, N.Y. 10110
W. W. Norton & Company Ltd., 37 Great Russell Street, London WC1B 3NU

1 2 3 4 5 6 7 8 9 0

For my wife Betty, thankfully:

God only fears one arrow: God's image, made human by Eve.
Now, archer in the marrow, stretch your own birth-cord's bow.
                    —Son of Man (in "Down" cycle)

Contents

PART TWO

PART THREE

PART ZERO REPLAYED

* * *

Acknowledgments

The following periodicals have published excerpts appearing in this book: *Agenda* (London), *Agni Review, American Spectator, A Review* (Amherst), *Atlantic Monthly, Beyond Baroque, Boston University Journal, Boxspring* (Hampshire College), *Chicago Tribune Magazine* ("Today's Poets"), *Choomia:* New England Issue, *Confrontation, Critical Inquiry* (University of Chicago), *Dark Horse* (Cambridge, Mass.), *Epoch* (Cornell University), *Forum* (University of Houston), *Green River Review, Hamden-Sydney Poetry Review, Harvard Advocate, Harper's, Images, Kenyon Review, The Little Magazine* (Quest) (New York City), *The Literary Review* (Fairleigh Dickinson University), *Massachusetts Review* (University of Massachusetts), *Michigan Quarterly Review* (University of Michigan), *Minnesota Review,* the *Nation,* the *New Yorker,* the *New York Quarterly,* the *New York Times* (Op-Ed page), *Nimrod* (University of Tulsa), *Ontario Review* (Princeton University), *Original Sin* (Windham College), *Paris Review, Parnassus, Partisan Review, Poetry* (Chicago), *Poetry Now, The Poetry Review* (Poetry Society of America), *Prairie Schooner, Quadrant* (Australia), *Sewanee Review, Shenandoah* (Washington & Lee University), *Triquarterly* (Northwestern University), *Webster Review, Yankee.*

The appendix essay, "Form in Poetry: Would Jacob Wrestle with a Flabby Angel," appeared partly in *Critical Inquiry* (University of Chicago), December 1978, and partly in *Parnassus,* Fall 1986; the poem closing this appendix essay, "Portrait of the Artist as an Old Dog," winner of the Varoujan Prize of the New England Poetry Club, appeared in *The Poetry Review* (Poetry Society of America), Spring 1985.

The author thanks these three journals for the right to reprint.

The lungfish quotation from P. Lieberman, *The Biology and Evolution of Language,* Harvard University Press, Cambridge, 1984, is reprinted with permission of Harvard University Press. The poetry quoted from Colin Reid, *Open Secret,* Colin Smythe Ltd., Gerrards Cross, Buckinghamshire, 1985 is with permission of Ben L. Reid, the copyright holder.

The circle-dot motif was borrowed (though altered) from this couplet by Angelus Silesius (1657):

> *Ich weiss nicht was ich bin / ich bin nit was ich weiss:*
> *Ein ding und nit ein ding / ein stüpffchin und ein kreiss.*

The "How dark the veins" stanza in the "Towards" cycle is not original but from the author's translation of the poem "Letzte Wache" (Final Vigil) by the German expressionist Georg Heym. In "Transitions," the phrase "become who you are" will be recognized as Nietzsche's.

The twenty-year project of these Applewood cycles, 1967–1987, could not have been completed without the ideal working conditions provided by the MacDowell Colony and by the Virginia Center for the Creative Arts.

Incalculable is my debt to the patience and wisdom of my Norton editor, Kathleen Anderson, who had to endure over a decade of continuous cutting and rewriting.

ARCHER IN THE MARROW

Identification of Speakers

We thinke that Paradise and Calvarie,
Christ's Crosse and Adam's tree, stood in one place;
Looke Lord, and finde both Adams met in me.
                                              —Donne

The text divides into "cycles," circling around the same central choices:
whether to make a Cross or a liberating arrow from the wood of the
knowledge tree, and whether to see man as a thing, determined totally
by things, or as self-surpassing. Each cycle expands its scope into the
next but can also be read as a separate poem. What unites them is the
same three speakers throughout, the voices of the father God and his
son being the imagined inner voices of the human "you" of today.

KEY TO WHO SPEAKS WHEN

Margin shifts and italics indicate speaker. FATHER: left-hand
margin. SON: indented to the right (not indented in cycles where
father is absent). Father and son—in alternate sections—hold
dialogues with YOU, the voice in italics and quotes. A dash in a
line is for change of speakers; Roman numerals head father's sections, Arabic the son's. Order of appearance in each dialogue is
listed after its heading; for example, 3. (you, then son).

Like the pronoun, YOU is of different sex and number according to
context; being American, YOU is still evolving, still fluctuating

erratically from cycle to cycle. FATHER is voicing the old universal thunder God, the brutality of reality, masked by the jauntiness of a stand-up-comic Mephisto. SON, as if in a Second Coming, now seeks to replace "Christian love" with two older opposites—Hebraic, Hellenic.

A fourth presence, mostly voiceless, is EVE, in the ever-changing roles associated with woman: Magdalen in the first cycle, Aphrodite in the last. Hers is what here is called the "transfiguring" or this-worldly magic of earth gods (small "g"), at war with the "transcending" or otherworldly magic of sky's Christian God. Also present and mostly voiceless is the Asian-Greek vine god, DIONYSUS, annually hacked and regreening, here seen as SON's lost half, two opposite brothers who complete each other.

These pages are poem, not tract and not play. The few stage directions are mainly for atmosphere. "Round" and "Gods" are the only two cycles that various experimental theaters have found stageable.

In the back of the book there is a glossary of foreign phrases, classical, Biblical, and historical references. The footnotes were written by the author at the publisher's request.

Motifs

Eden's forbidden appletree of knowledge lit man's eyes with consciousness; it is the same applewood (according to medieval legend) from which Christ's cross is carved. As both showman and toymaker, "father" wants to keep his troublesome human toy a blank-eyed "thing." But the awakening toy is straining to be more than a thing, to expand from dot into circle. Hence man's duel with God at Land's End, where the book both starts and ends. On that very beach, a mutant "rogue" gene first beached man's fishy forebear, resulting in lungs and then in brow. When "you" (modern mankind, whether female or male) are about to lose your duel, the shape-changing vineyard god, Dionysus-Bacchus, stows you away in timeless Part Zero. There you witness, as inescapable seasonal circles, the parallel yet different deaths of the nailed son and the hacked wine god.

Returning in Part One to today's reality, you now go spiraling through your eighteen concentric "cycles," each one the battlefield of a particular one-syllable title, such as Waltz, Bread, Salt, Stain. The Waltz cycle pounds forth the 1-2-3 timing (birth-spawn-death: here "dumped, dunked, done") in which father has jailed all life. Guided by the Son of Man, you try to escape the three-step: not by ethereal transcending (the New Testament that "son" now repudiates) but by a transfiguring-yet-earthbound deepening of step two into a fourth step only lovers attain. No easy solutions: in the Bread cycle of Part I for example, you discover that a twentieth-century wallowing in fleshpots is no more liberating than Victorian pots of spirit.

In Parts II and III, father keeps his toys robotized, their apple-knowledge blinkered, by luring them to soar beyond that human frailty which is their true strength. Overreaching toward impossible super-human purities, they fall into subhuman bestialities, culminating in the "red hands" of the Auschwitz and Toward cycles. In the Mek cycle the materialist solutions of the latest technology prove as nightmarish as the spiritual ones.

"Part Zero Replayed'" gropes for a third way. Gods being your own projections, only man's free choice can combine earth's Hellenic and Hebraic halves, Dionysus with Jesus, Aphrodite with Eve: thereby man can perhaps free himself and them from the script writer in the sky. Throughout (till the rival halves merge), Christ's sacrificial-lamb motif is at war with the erotic goatfoot-imprint of Greek paganism. And also throughout, "the hill" refers mostly to Christ's uphill climb to his crucifixion on Mount Golgotha, but occasionally to Olympus, the hill of the Greek gods.

In the "Like Boaz" Prologue of Part III, the indictment of sky's gene-scripting patriarch reaches its climax in the Eve-Aphrodite out-burst of the feminine "you," and a new Armageddon is looming, launched by the key "Applewood Ballad" of the "Threads" cycle. With such high stakes and after absorbing a painful new lesson from each cycle, both son and you "replay," in the end, their earlier choices. Not till then (last cycle, last page) does the meaning of the book's title word, "Archer," fully emerge.

Meanwhile, ignoring these squabbles of mere gods, earth's first lungfish keeps popping up unexpectedly: your time-traveling great-grandfather. Bearing the flukey "rogue" gene of cycle six, he launches—by quitting the sea—the motif of "selfsurpass" for his human descen-dants. From his discovery of lungs comes not only the breathing of air and the invasion of land but that sky-invading weapon known as human song. With the formcraft of song and art, mortal flesh poaches crea-tivity from its Creator; hence, that other recurrent theme, those ancient painted cave walls of Cro-Magnon man at Lascaux in Dordogne.

As for motifs of formcraft, this requires a quick background com-ment about poetry itself. The blood of the poet is what blood banks call "Rh positive"; his is the twofold Rh of rhyme and rhythm; together they are his rhapsody, his rhaps-ody, his (in Greek) "ode-stitching." In the ballet of words, rhyme is the *pas de deux* of mated contraries; rhythm is Time in leotards.

Rhymes are also the punctuation marks of rhythm, its quick tiptoe commas or else its colons, long-voweled and slow. For rhyme's coupling function, the substitute may be the recurrence of image, breath, alliteration, or other motif. For rhythm there is no substitute. And rhythm—not as artificial convention but as iambic heartbeat or variously accented sinew-flow—is flesh language. The swords of the book's dueling voices are rhythms, not creeds.

Most rhymed poetry rhymes only the line's end, causing it to be overaccented. When rhyming a line's first syllable with an end syllable (as in "Lids" in the "Eyes" cycle), the aim is to discover "ode-stitchings" more interwoven and rhymes newborn. The resonance of a living (not mechanical) rhyme—body-rooted, not dead formalist—has an eerie Eden earliness, as if April had just been invented and no bird sang before.

* * *

As backdrop motif, the basic setting, here and throughout, has a ceiling meathook and two big canvases: Rembrandt's "Slaughtered Ox," Van Eyck's "Adoration of the Lamb." Rolling up their sleeves purposefully, father and son set up these props. Here and throughout, they are addressing not each other but their human begetter (the italicized you-voice). To this "you" they now address—as the curtain rises—their leitmotif quatrains:

    1. (son)
    Toys don't know they're toys.
    If they do, they're not.
    A thing or not a thing?
    A circle or a dot?

I. (father)
When dots are circles, staring back,
And yes affirms them less than no,
When down gets uppity and up swings low,
Not till then can heaven crack.

    2. (son)
    My father who looks aside
    Assumed blank faces on the toys he tried.

I have learnt different, being sent inside.
In autumn only man is heavy-eyed.

II. (father)
Your father who takes no side
Faces the eighth day satisfied.
But what if toys look up less blank than lizards?
Next time I'll make man button-eyed.

3. (son, then you in dialogue)
My father who wrote the play
Assumes a plaything is a thing for play.
"Did he send you as his spy into my pulse-beat?"
I am defecting to the side of clay.
    (Son hangs two placards: one from Pindar, 'The joy-god Diony-
    sus, star and root,' and one from *Revelation* of St. John, 'I Jesus,
    root and star.')
"Sky's. God. reaps. grim."—Clay's Dionysus twines
The joyous reapers, the enjoyed ripe fruit.
"Forbidden fruit?"—Till ripened. Call him night root
And morning star: dark wine-press, dawn-clear wines.

*"Sky's God reaps prim; is it true he made
Demons of certain daughters of soil and sea?"*
Your foamborn queen? And your loamborn Eden mate?
Not demons—refugees; the demon he.
    (Son replaces placards with paintings: Cranach's Eve with apple,
    Botticelli's sea birth of Aphrodite. You addressing the paint-
    ings:)
*"If a cross is but lumber God borrows
From a tree that's untouchably God's,
If Eve's but an exile God harrows
From the greenest of all the world's woods,
If the foamborn ghost in our marrows
Is but frozen, awaiting spring floods,
Can we carve warm applewood arrows to arm
Touchable gods?"*

III. (father to you)
Never. Not till Eve comes strolling back,

Spitting apple pits, new orchards in her wake.
Not till, in Foamborn's wake, your lost sea-home
Gives Lamb goatfeet, gives dust loam.
    (father to stagehands, confidently)
Angels, stop lolling on that pin—come quick
And wilt two queens.
    (father alone, anxiously)
Just now what goatfoot nicked
All village greens?

Showdown on Land's End

Iced marsh; sere meadow. Sign: ALLHALLOWS EVE. Only two voices:
father and you. One seagull watching intently.

I. (father, then you)
Seaside and bleak; where all last duels are.
"Tunes warmer on winds waywarder—"
Land's End; your lungfish ancestor
Here first slurped air.
"But now—" —You've come a long way,
Ape baby. —*"Now man and you,*
Having. it. out." —And the blue gone gray.
And no shape-changing trickster. —*"Vine always around."*
Kind of late; green gone yellow; no watcher at all—
"Only some gull in the dusk-lull."
Then what are you up to, so chummy with winds?
Picking up feathers to make yourself wings?
"He always—." —No rescue this round.
"Tunes warmer on winds waywarder than others
When from the frozen graves the marshfires glow
Bring me—." —A three-step from your fathers' fathers,
Kicking warm heels against their jails of snow.
"Waltz-beats? In swamp-churn what avails

Decorum?" —Better not know.
"Some heels look almost shaggy through the ice."
Better not look down, if vertigo—
"It goes right through me—I feel it between my thighs—
That scrape of claws from under their roof of ice."
Their roof: your floor.
"Both lure
Each other. Of course, I'd never dance on ice.
. . . Unless the marshfire guides me safe." —But if
Ignis fatuus also guides a jailbreak, then . . .
"Some graves are made to waltz on." —On,
Or in. —*"Stop: what's that beast-cage whiff*
Of furry copulations just below?"
What's earthmom? Step 2—gap 2—
Takes two. —*"If my birth was step 1—"*
Step 3 is the tomb gape: you've tripped on
Your family crypt. —*"Not mine! Each now alone.*
I've shed my dead."
They're back for trick-or-treat. They haven't shed
You. —*"Let me go."* —Their return from ice
Isn't quite birth, but . . . ? —*"Glow? I hope only marsh glow."*
Allhallows was once not pranks but ghostly flicker.
"Something lower's crawling nearer quicker. Let me go."
If on your grave of many a death ago
You slip on ice—
"I'll waltz with decorum. Let me—." —If from the moat
Your own buried claws—. —*"I feel at my throat*
Hot ice."

Interruption; a gull shrieks (the wine-god watcher, the "shape-changing trickster"); man's debacle cut short by watcher catapulting you into timeless Part Zero, where you will hear son at Golgotha and hear Dionysus at vineyard.

PART ZERO

(Outside Time)

Part Zero is frozen outside time and space. Speakers
(watched by silent you) in three ever-repeated monologue cycles: son,
Dionysus, son.

CYCLE ONE:

Up

———————

"Is not the body on the Cross the apple [of perilous choice] *restored to its tree?"*

    —W.A. Murray, "What Was the Soul of the Apple?"
    Essential Articles for the Study of John Donne's Poetry

"There were also women looking on afar off: among whom was Mary Magdalene."

    —Mark, 15:40

———————

Lone speaker of all cycle one is trudging uphill; oddly crowned; bent by an unseen weight. Bare landscape except for a stunted olive tree and an oversize cactus. Looking on afar off: two Marys.

———————

1.
Uphill;
Sometimes I fell;
Reached up for thirty years,
Then thirty years were up.
Fell, but fell never down: no tired dawdles
(I then, I then still called the loamed 'the mired')
On fallen petals. . . .
Soapboxers and gods tend to end up uphill.
But not all mounts are sermons; one,

Tempting me with This World, failed. Another nailed.
I, haggard under more than sun,
Lugged more than weight. Dung beetles staggered under
The moldered skulls. I shouldered what I shouldered.

2.
Skull Hill was so scuffed a rug that the threads unmeshed;
My reach fleshed out too late,—a leper's hug.
A doll was playing with a winsome lass
Elsewhere;
Glass ponds in scarves were skating a wee lad,
Not here.
Here on Skull Hill, no chubby grass;
The dogs were fetid, it's the air went mad.
Rome's Kraut centurions sweated out their north.
They gave me—I thought it was water—gall,
Or was it (time swirling me back and forth)
Gas? Mad air,
Were you fooling around with my shower stall?
And back here on the hill was the heat already a breath
From my second death,[1] from my far
Chimney's Baal-bellied belch?[2]
No, it was still my first Passion play; Bethlehem's star
Had not yellowed into a badge.

3.
It was my first; the replay still whirled in time's funnel,
A world of Pilates the stagehands,

                              hands of ablution
At the two Solutions solving my chosenness: first
The Friday one, then the Final.
Skull Hill was a scorpion so dry that the grass claws
Crunched; I was treading straw stairs. The sting was
That straight lines are round and a treadmill a clause
Of my contract with immortality.
Then take away this cup from me,
This cornucopia cup.
Uphill or up wood, always my jig is up.

Even my ashes, a Santa Claus
In reverse, even they chimney up.
But wait, my two death-dance orbits—they hadn't come close
Yet, it still was my first.
Judenstern and Nativity were not yet a binary star
Writing me straight in crooked lines

                          that jar men's doze
Almost (and almost God's, his snoring worst).

4.
But back from time's helter-skelter, still here on the hill,
My all-seeing eyes, up here in the first play's welter,
Foresaw
       nothing. Was my blinder my Elder
Mary's brow-sheltering hand?
I then, I then still doubted my brow-branding Other:
Young Mary, my Eva, rekindling my embering
Vision, long shackled by shelter.
On that Friday of death's birthday,
Hooded in that hilltop swelter,
Stood both Marys of my earth-stay;
Stabat Mater.
But Other—where's Other?—I lost sight of Other's
Red hair in a sandtrap that three rival brothers
(Calling it Holy Land) each made cacophonous
With mutual anathemas' brotherly love.
Crusaders as locusts, sand hatching their thunder,
Swarmed round her young head where no melody guards;
Where no flowering guides, she fled under.
(Is she waiting, harassed by Saharas,
Where numbed loam goads?)
My Elder was beautiful, bearing human-scale cares,
But when she wore all the world's grief,
Was she still, was she still our protectress
Or blubbering gelder of all of us, all
                          godforsaken gods?
(Where's Other, tousled with all petals fallen since Eve?)
. . . But here, back here in the high hot glade,

When I sought shade in soul,
I heard a gnarled old cactus
Scornfully growl,
And from his lion-crouch came loping
(King-beast of Golgothas)
Thirst. Sand
Seeped through my rags, I. . . my. . . own. . . hourglass.
Mournfully wafting white theories at gray human practice,
I sent out doves, preened spotless as my Book;
Watch my brow be olive-branch crowned!
Came a drumbeat of wings, no cooing sound;
Came a carrion stench;
White crows came back.
My bare brow blenched: what's in that beak,
What whitewash is darker than black?
O why did their taunting talons clench
Branches brambly and round?
Has God-crown turned out to be thistle?
Then it's 'mire' of Eva that's flower:
Portals of hairy gristle, petals of delicate fire.
To our frailty—sharing and pardon,
To loneness—tellurian feasts:
Eve's human-scale garden, not God's scale nor beast's.

5.
If her garden's as mussed as a brine-drenched dress,
Five-fingered caress by the senses,
Was I wrongly 'right' when I dyed love white
To bleach my own frenzies?
I stared for answers where Jerusalem still
Floated, mirage or home, beneath my hill
And saw
            man's wriggliest question marks
Floating like sidelocks of my patriarchs.
One question mark wiggled its fishhook around me:
For loving too high, had love crowned me high
With a dunce cap that tickled

Me bloody? Sometimes I fell
(Watermilkmotheryourhand).

6.
This was the March it rained so little
The olive groves were crisp with dust.
I, too, was brittle crust, my blood
Hemorrhaged by doubt as theirs by drought.
Linked by our upward-straining un-sereneness,
The woods that watched me carrying the wood
Had years ago kept green my desert years,
But now the blink of noon—the Eye had seen us—
Parched our last climb (save for two women's tears)
And led me toward a
                    tree nest. After
I fell the third time, Easter,
Waiting ahead for all dry groves, gave
Up,—ebbing
Their tree blood, ebbing
My greenness,
              except one crest.
Triumph! My crest (but why, young Mary, no fruit?)
Transcended laps of loam for sky-high cleanness.
. . . Triumph? I failed—I fell (crest drained the root)
Uphill.

CYCLE TWO:

Hacked

———————

The character of the 'mysterious smiling heartless Stranger' [in Euripides,
The Bacchae] *who came out of the east, disquiets the mind: divine in
some manifestations . . . and the shadow of imposture falls upon some.
Pentheus called him 'a foreign wizard'; he may have been nothing more,
but he sent the women of Thebes to rave and dance upon the hills, and he
had the still more perilous gift of* self-intoxication.
—E. M. Butler, *The Myth of the Magus*

*Dionysus-Bacchus was the vine which is always pruned—as nothing else
that bears fruit; every branch cut away. . . . Like Persephone . . . who
also rose from the dead, . . Dionysus died with the coming of the cold.
Unlike her, his death was horrible; he was torn to pieces. He was the
tragic god.*
—Edith Hamilton, *Mythology*

*As god of earth Dionysus belongs like Persephone to the world below as
well as above. . . . In connection with the death of vegetation in winter
. . . he was called Zagreus ('Torn-in-pieces').*
—Dictionary of Classical Antiquities

———————————————————————

Scene: vineyard. Cycle two has two sections: spring, then autumn. Son of
Man speaks first section, "Good." In long section 2, "To My Gatherer," son
and you—both silent—are overhearing an unseen Asian stranger addressing
an unseen farm girl.

The most familiar parallels of seasonal sacrifice and regrowth include Persephone-Proserpine re-ascending from Pluto's Hades, Isis regathering the fourteen strewn pieces of Osiris, and the grapes renewing the hacked vine-limbs of Dionysus-Bacchus. Persephone's mother is the crops-and-fertility goddess Demeter-Ceres (whence "cereals").

Isis becomes pregnant with renewed sun by straddling the erect corpse of murdered Osiris: in Egypt god of inseminating waters and in Greece equated with the "torn-in-pieces" vine god. Both countries knew him as also "the many-faced," the tricky shape-juggler: plant, seagull, prince with leopards.

---

1. (son: *Good*)
In the month of March the snails climb tender trees
To be nearer the Pleiades.
Grass fingers nab heat.
The fish jump for the fun of it.
Later the roses are willing to fall.
The wasted thistle-fluff isn't sorry at all.
A vineyard, met while walking, is a shelter
Good to hold to in that helter-skelter.
For fun—or baited hooks?—life likes to twitch;
After the ice, it will not matter which.
After the ice, the feathers—once all throat—
Are shushed; the paraplegic lakes can not reach out.

And so, from hooked exuberance to numbed retreat,
The gamuts have no meaning; or what they have of it
Encysts in chunky particulars,—
The specific timothy-grass, the ungeneralized tears,
The vineyard met while walking, a life-buoy of here,
Good to hold, in wave on wave of anywhere.

2. (traveling stranger's voice from vineyard to farm girl: *To My Gatherer*)
They're deft, his hit-men, but I've foiled frost's prowess
Six months—not bad—with scarves of foliage. Even
When his red sports-hearse zaps me—fall's his season—
Your warmth outflanks his morgue's Plutonian powers.

His half-time moll, you sulk in dead soil's innards,
Beauty queen of his winter-carnival pageant.
Betray his underground; dear double agent,
Trigger the annual comeback of the vineyards.

But don't demean us; don't, Cereal's daughter, mete us
Her pep-talk crackle, the waked year's breakfast cornflake.
Pop us a crocus, March's first green mandrake,
Kicking soil's belly like a furious fetus.

Tough midwife Ceres, that belly underfoot,
Rips forth no pastoral of doves and loves,
No dainty-gauzy primavera fête;
This sweaty murderess treads red screaming leaves.

Are we daubed with 'life' by mortician-crayons
Of seasonal frostbite and seasonal blazons?
Tombed daughter, save us from such salvations;
Once flout your cycle, *reverse* the play once:

Carve pine from mast, eke grapes from raisins.

* * *

Not leaf's—a loftier treading—grape's renascence,
That's what your prunings promised my impatience.
When maenad groupies snatched me from the Asians,
I risked the terrible jump of all creations:—

Wine's jump from its own skin into the . . . where?
Into abysses? These honor—they raise back up—
Art that outleaps its artist. O spill-and-gather
Me in soused future's cup.

Self-soused you call me? Test my bard-bravado.
Riding the same ill wind by which I'm riven,
I'm the one spore to make your fallow meadow
Hum with the humus of remembered rhythm.

And anyway, who cares how much frost shuffled
My ripped-off wrappers—fanning forth from man
To worm and back, through spore's accordion span—
So long as rogue-gene smirks within, unruffled.

Don't you smirk too; I know I'm all awry.
I'm fluff, I stick to every whim like lint.
I'm dandelion fuzz: my gold spikes dry
And silver off with every aimless wind.

I wear what glistens (next round, I'll leap as trout).
My motes traipse far—I gawk from every spark.
I rocket from smokestacks, intersect with soot,
And stun noon's sauna with my sunnier dark.

True, I'll admit my quicksilver's hard to fathom.
Agreed, my hashed-up selves have hushed my thunder.
My words—these leaves that pelt your downstairs slumber—
Pall. To your frost-numbed ears I seem a phantom.

Seem. Yet made flesh by touching. Must I pinch you
(Already I've sloughed a hand back) to convince you?
When I laugh back a leg or two, I'll lurch
Back as spring's springboard. Watch my dead bones launch

Your mulch's liveliest crocus-fling next March.

             *   *   *

Once more the wheel advances
Us back to fall's last parch.
Come twine—before these branches
Shed whiter avalanches—

Our brief uncolorfast dances under fall's last daubed arch.

Stroll to the ducklings' pond we once found peaceful.
Kick off your sandals, wade among toy ships.
Lend me the trust I'll forfeit. Fear no evil.
For the first hour we'll just touch fingertips.

Fall's afterglow and mine can't help but forfeit,
Tomorrow's wind being chill, the trust you covet.
Then glean from loss (feel pond's foreboding ripple?)
One day that's larger than the year is little.

Clouds blown but not yet jostling and contentious;
Some wings not yet pushed south; some plums still clinging:
While there's one sun-warmed seat on these cool benches,
Lean back—inhale the last bloom's lingering.

Lean open today to the day I've wrestled from winter.
Green skirts get stained white anyhow tomorrow,
No procreant flow of plow but barren snow.
Fruit needs us needing each other; today I'm your kindler—

—and trickster,
                    and tricked: the chore of getting me torn
Hurts worse each round. To pry your hips from ice,
Must I play corpse? O then play Isis on
My impudent thighs.

My Bacchus credentials, these leopards[1] I lure,
You see them tugging my cart?
Unnatural? More tricks? All the truer
(Ask Pentheus) my art.

Shrubs taunt me: 'Gnarled old stump, lopped bare and limbless,
Where's now the grape-wreathed dandy of Olympus?'
Doze a solstice too long when patching my fourteen shapes,
And no more grapes.

                    *   *   *

Across the acres and eras we slough like husk,
I hurtle through mask after mask to your pheromone musk.
Not scorched but phoenixed by that moist flame, I press
Vulgar hands beneath whatever your era's dress.

Without antiphonal vulgarities,
No tide. From when the buds enfold the bees

Till the last closing of the plowshare's furrow,
Your furlow ebbs; then back to Pluto's burrow.

Your tide? Who'll bridge its lace and its typhoon,
The fragile moonbeam and the frenzied moon?
I, human-scale god, not God, it's I who've cut
The veil between love's flesh and flesh-in-rut.

*   *   *

A Son of man—he's listening—once my brother—
Went slumming as decoy for a slumlord father.
Men throng to stroke—in father shepherd's shed—
A lamb. They'll find a bull with lowered head.

If—one son torn, One nailed—our brotherly war ends,
Unsnarling burrs of dogma from our garlands,
If east and East^2 reverse west's icy rout,
Father watch out.

We whelps of God: as mulch for spring's
Jack-in-the-box, we're ladderlessly chained
Below. But what when we two, blending, bend
Chains into rungs?

Then writhe, old worm of the star ditch,
In the Milky Way slime of your skin,
Trailing empty white vastness, vast in vain when
Dense earth's out of reach.

They said, 'We must duel near water'—'water,' the earthlings called.
They said, 'We feel salt stinging'—the brine in them yanked by the salt.
The showdown with the Showman must end where the show began:
Land's End again.

Beach; I, spying as sea bird; when the scions
Of lungfish duel with God, they'll need a god's alliance.
That hour I'll be my brother—no, he'll be me, my heathen
Gull wings bursting dovecotes Galilean.

*   *   *

Or am I nothing but bones from urns Aegean?
Or puppet of some homesick modern's paean?
But whether you're goddess of farms or farmer's daughter,
Hear what I, wine-dream's traveling salesman, offer:—

Flesh being gene-scrawled for neither music nor justice,
Let's improvise them, no matter what the script is.
Parching on Scylla or drowning on Charybdis,
We're Proteus dodging blueprints of Procrustes.

I'm flow^3; you can't step twice in the same me.
You're grow; a thousand winters freeze in vain.
Towns rinse their stinking dentures in our holy
Shared tide; we couldn't care less; we bloom from stain.

Your globe-size bell of clay (the sun your sexton,
Ringing your seasons) tolls my vintage home;
Could I but voice the clangor of a claxon,
I'd fell whole cities on your seismic loam.

You, gentler, salvage what Octobers topple,
A plum twig or a storm-plucked mallard plume.
Enfold me in the corduroys I rumple,
Your robe of corrugated sag and zoom.

Fused by brine's aphrodisiac aroma,
We—time's *noyades*—drown with a warm defiance,
The way the beached momentum of a comber
Once tossed a fish^4 whose lung would dent sky's silence.

* * *

Enough of grandeurs. It's now grotesques I'll mimic.
I'm a wallow of toads; I'm a gamboling wart-hog, preening
Garbage-crowned bristles. When a god's descending,
Descent knows no limit.

From gross abyss, I'll then climb lace cascades,
Whatever's wisped or pendant,

Ear lobes or dew, a trellis of ivies or braids,
A comet-mane[5] ascendant

Above grief's cypress . . . till I'm an air-vine named
'Flowering Nostalgia'; rooted firm in cloud,
My petals droop their pity on earth's maimed
Sky-hopes as shroud.

*   *   *

I'll tell you what 'life' is: water compressed by form.
Four billion years of cooped-up soup ago,
A first cell joined a second. But we earth-warm
Sprouters reap frost. In fall the glue lets go.

Too much sugar in these grapes, too gorged their ripeness:
My green seeps off in their blue balloons of ferment.
So filled with fullness, doom swells predetermined
Between the August warming and the winepress;—

So deep in summer is not far from fall.

*   *   *

I used to get reborn from fall.
Not rind—the core's outworn this fall.
Rainfall's forlorn refrain:
'The torn stays torn this fall.'

Your months below were sometimes slow. But you came back.
Was last time longer? Pluto stronger? But you came back.
This time delayed? Your yawns of late? But you'll come back.
My foliage? Red. My crest? Half dead. (She not quite back?)

Are vine limbs (yearly hacked for next year's wine)
Me when you patch them, or is vine but vine?
If it's no error to Easter a flower, what shame
In doing as much for me? And whether your nickname

Is Isis or Magdalen or Persephone
And mine Osiris or Bacchus, let's feel flattered,
Not bored. Why are you snoring? Don't dare shed me;
We'll either be two phantoms or one body;—

I'm just as real as you are . . . merely scattered.

CYCLE THREE:
Round

The world's great age begins anew,
The golden years return.
—Shelley

The wings return into the bird to nail him.
—Paul Eluard

The patient does not remember *anything of what he has forgotten and*
repressed, but acts *it out. He reproduces it not as a memory but as an*
action; he repeats it without, of course, knowing he is repeating it.
—Freud

This cycle has only one speaker, unidentified and so eccentric that he incites
a silent visitor against an ordinary-looking cocoon on an ordinary-looking
branch. Bungling of the sabotage darkens the sky over all old and new road-
builders and triggers the unintended chain reaction that follows. (No you,
no father, no Dionysus in this son cycle.)

TIME: tomorrow but twenty centuries ago.

PLACE: Los Angeles but ancient Tarsus, home of Saint Paul (he doesn't
appear) in Romanized metic-Greek Asia Minor.

SETTING: incongruous mix of ancient and Californian props.

PLACARDS: "SPQR"; "WELCOME TO TARSUS"; "THIS WAY TO
DISNEYLAND"; "ROMANS, GO HOME—NO NUKES IN EDEN";
"DRINK REV. JONES'S KOOL-AID HOLY WATER."

---

1. (Toga'd speaker is addressing own trousered reflection in big distorting
   funhouse-mirror, while stumbling against branch with oversized cocoon.)
Stop
Stumbling; you might wake up
Something. So you've come sight-seeing
From the edge of our good-old-flat earth? By Mithra,
You togaless tourists from America
Dress odd. . . . Say, what's this mess?
   (Points at cocoon; it emits slow droning.)
To peel (like an . . . an . . . apple) unripe moth,
Speeds hatching up. Toward wings? Toward death?
   (faster droning)
Can there be fruit that picks its picker?
Cast from the slingshot of the past,
This fruit-egg's out of sync with time's slow flicker.
Suppose it's you it aims at, aims . . . into:
Would its dank wings make your shocked shoulders bulge?
   (Cocoon pulsates twice.)
Would it—would sprouting silkworm sludge—
Feel loathsome to you or delicious? Stay
Sane, don't answer. WELCOME TO L.A.

2. (During blackout, Asian and Californian props get reversed. From now
   on, cocoon sways violently with every shift of time or role.)
If east-west landmarks keep kind of swaying,
It's a smog mirage. WELCOME (as I was saying)
TO TARSUS: a salubrious clime,
Famed for its bath of sulphur slime;
As a Jaycee—(J.C.?)—I boost our local trade.
   (shrill outburst)
But not some greasy foreign fad,
Some meshuga Christian with chutzpa, spoiling the neighborhood
Real estate price. We Romans—that gossip Judas lies
When he says I speak Aramaic at home.
I'm pure Romanized Metic Greek.
When mumso took me to my first crucifixions,
I also enjoyed the popcorn and balloons.
   (hiding hands)

The holes in my palms, they're only sores from oars.
    (anxious glance at wall clock, suddenly ticking louder)
Blame smog dust if the proconsul asks why we're late.
Then watch the old fool wheeze,
'Behead the aedile of Los Angeles.'
Dust's what we Roman Europeans hate.
    (Floor wobbles; lights reverse colors; voice-reversal from Rotarian to vatic.)
We Asians whom young Rome would 'modernize'
With soap and floppy disks—our dust shall rise
With dragon wings and blot out western skies:
The savage joy of it, our home-brewed witchcraft, our sublime
Cults conk our conquerors. But . . . Caesar's spies . . .
    (looking over shoulder)
I mean: our home-brewed wine—sublime!
Our Asian loyalty to Rome—yes, that's what is sublime.
Call us provincials, but our eclogues rhyme,
And PanAm triremes bring your *Times* on time.
    (Clock's hour hand speeds up furiously.)
Time! Ticking faster! Wings hatch with one more tick;
    (yelling at his mirror image)
Don't let them stretch, abort them quick.

3. (Speaker gathers pulsing cocoon into paper hanky, dumps it in garbage
    can.)
This garbaged fetus clawing pudgily
Coffee grounds and eggshells, pail of history,
This hedgehog huddle of lewd complicity
Making its dumpers wonder if they won:
Eyelids a senile dawn has wizened,
Still dazed at half-becoming what it isn't:
One gut-smeared snot rag holds it all.
    (Speaker winces fastidiously, then shakes chiding finger at mirror,
    attributing his own dumping action to visitor.)
You! —stop being squeamish when duty and hygiene call.
How shoddy of the grosser category
To die in ways that make the nobler sorry:
Like nailed on a cr—. . . no, cross it out quick;
Slip of the tongue; I meant stuck on a stick.
    (to creature in can)

Thou shouldst have played Saint Francis to hyenas,
Preached to piranhas, stroked lions in arenas,
Not come unarmed to man.
    (to mirror again)
Are you some milkshop monk of the Certosa
To flinch—almost throw up—at what you've done?
Would Darwin wince like a mimosa
Each time some bug-eyed *via dolorosa*
Lands its unfitness in a can?
Now nail it down to stop its gucky throb.
Nothing's as squirmy as an unfanged specter's
Hilarious gum-nips at its vivisectors
When grubs rush in to batten on a blob.
    (spearing it and again attributing his actions to mirror visitor)
Ecce homunculus! —upon a matchstick,
His side speared by a cocktail-cherry toothpick.
This lepidopterous preposterous clown—
We're safe now—might have brought an empire down.
    (long silence, then noise from garbage)
What droning churns the mess, what breeze blows colder?
The slingshot catapulting this cocoon
From Manger to cluttered can
Could not foresee a comedown so bizarre:
Hunching one horribly-sprouting shoulder
Deep in a quilt of Hershey bar,
This . . . what?—not moth? not child?—this splinter-crowned
Christ-dragon, squished into a ketchup jar.
Well, this is it, the end of faith
Demons. Yes, squish it more, you've rescued earth.
This ir-re-vers-ible god-crash, it's the death—
Oh no, you've triggered it—the wings, the birth
Of myth.
    (Smoke-wings rise from can; speaker's fist cracks mirror.)
My stumbling new-world bungler, you've. been. shed.

4. (as wings, now enormous, blot out ceiling-lamp 'sun')
There it flies, the self I fled,
The slingshot pebble, now a looming boulder

Dooming all empire. Twenty centuries older,
My incense-smoke still goads the heart's hot smolder
Against cold Roman roads.
An Asian war[1] drags on, the legions molder;
A burglar Caesar[2] quits as office holder;
Pop oracles make shamans bolder;
The day two hounded boat people[3] find no bed
For their baby's head, can Manger and Star be far?
When slum child's rattle bloats to bishop's crozier,
Full circle—*in hoc signo*—closes closer,
And the catacomb lets the empire steal the Star.
At last (to finish Gibbon's yellowed folder)
The Tiber matron lets the hired soldier
In, Declines
         him for a while,
                and Falls.

5. (to audience)
Eden's and autumn's and empire's: threefold falls.
The waste hurts most in all the falls I've faced,
The waste of you, of us: man moving motionless fast
In a merry-go-round on a quaky playground whose San
Andreas fault is . . . man.
I've let—to stop the ride—a soldier spear my side;
It didn't stop. We spiraling down, not up,
Why can't we change (*plainte éternelle, plainte éternelle*)
The wooden zebras of our carousel?
No sooner said than—. Already we're all . . . elsewhen.
   (Floor tilts, lamps blink.)
And while new earth gets busy getting born,
Watch me adorn the ceiling—now a screen—
With reruns of each famous scene
From your old script, now scrapped.
   (Speaker aims projector at stage's blue ceiling;
   slides of familiar history follow.)
Call sky a schoolbook; blue pages, flipping, show
The scenes you, yawning, already know.
Watch Columbus discover the earth is flat;

As he falls off the edge—see the bottomless vat?—
The sailors are jeering, 'We told you so.' . . .
See Charles the Anvil at Tours kiss Allah's rod;
Hear, ever since, Parisians speak
Euro-Arab slang with special chic. . . .
Pray to Our Lady Diamat among
The dreaming spires of age-old Trotskigrad. . . .
Cheer Sir Benedict being gracious to the throng
At Governor's Mansion in Arnoldston, D.C.;
Folks call him 'the father of our colony.' . . .
Adore Saint Lucrezia Borgia, first woman Pope. . . .
Now 1984^4; vast earth goes pop.
    (On stage a very small balloon pops.)
But we're all safe by now in neo-earth:
Man's second chance, new April's birth.
    (Screen now reverses endings; earth unflattened, Charles now the
    Hammer, Arnoldston now Washington, etc.)
Atoms, change partners; reverse your spin.
Rejoice—out's in—neurosis is new roses.
And each new Sacred Wood
    (sudden tone of infinite weariness)
Still ends as gallows wood.
Each time we switch sky's tape
    (pointing at projector)
We all escape on Noah's
Titanic. Our ship rides a Möbius strip;
Though we're free to choose either side for our trip,
There's not much April in sky's comic strip.
    (Kicks projector off stage,)

6.
There's still much Rome. Rome leaves no dew on roses.
It's more than roads a road-maker bulldozes.
Even rococo (road gone procelain) is glad sadly;
And Big Brother Geometry adores sanity
Madly,
        painting straight strips of white on life's black whirls.
Possessed by System's demon pack,

The carousel zebras tread relentless wheels,
These Gadarene zebras, drowning in history.
   (to cracked mirror)
Peel off, peel off that hobbyhorse simile;
Beneath it who spins there? Road-maker Paul, are you me?
You're my ventriloquist, my sleep your Babel,
Presser of green who made dried leaves a Bible,
Presser of me.
   (addressing white throne, placarded as "HOUSE THAT PAUL BUILT:—
   Jan Bockelsen: Rev. Jim Jones. Torquemada: Robespierre. Calvin: Lenin.")
Paul, Paul, with your Saint Procrustes banner
Of 'infinite love through infinite terror,'[5]
Propaganda minister of God's second tome,
You bring me back the throne I'm racing from;
Two corpses shuttling threads that live,
You weave, I unweave (call it hist. of civ.)
The loom of Rise and Fall.
But I'm off to hide my throne from living eyes.

7. (Speaker spins clock backwards in time. Wing creature drops from ceil-
   ing, shrinks back into tree's cocoon.)
Backwards my centuries roll, like corpses' eyes.
With twenty spins of counterclockwise tick,
Made cunning by the fever spooled in me,
I shrink my dragon soul into a matchstick,
My misused throne into a tree.
Well hid from cult in woodwork's haystack;
No spear in my side; just cocktail-cherry's toothpick.
I've gouged green free of white god-rot; I've restored
The innocence of wood.
   (Cocoon on tree hums again, each droning followed by speaker-voice
   deepening, as if invaded by his own rejected and cocooned god-voice. His
   god-words are capitalized throughout.)
IT. WASN'T. EASY.—whose voice?—BEING—
Being what? Can't be; I've restored—
IT WASN'T EASY BEING GOD;
COMPASSION FESTERED WORSE THAN THORNS;
EMPATHY SPOILED THE CHISEL;

TO MAKE ME HUMAN WAS INHUMAN.
I'D RATHER SCULPTURE EXCREMENT THAN EGO;
WHEN MOBS SPREAD GODS, THE BLESSING IS BUBONIC;
OMNISCIENCE WASN'T WORTH THE LOSS OF WONDER.
Out, out, you voice I dread; to shed my cross's wood,
I've wooed a fool into a tree. My appletree.
WASN'T WORTH THE—. —Out! Or might the voice be me?
One foolproof escape: to my own source I'll turn:—

8. (spinning clock still farther back)
—the start of gods I'll burn burn burn,
The spooks who thought up men who thought up spooks.
Lean cheetahs whom my forest-fire slaughters,
Myth upon myth lopes by with backward looks.
Here's Ur, there's Stonehenge, up from boiling waters
Poseidon hurtles on the heels of Dagon;
Venus and Mars have always shared cremations;
Up north the *Götter* take their *Dämmerung* stations;
All blaze as brakelessly as Phaëthon's wagon.
Spin wilder; now's the moment, now I hide it—
My God plague—in some dawn-age dragon,
Sealed from man in some bug nest of prehistory.
Time curves? Watch my momentum override it.
My will be done; I have annulled my *agon;*
Right through creation's morning I'm riding free.
   (Straddles appletree branch and whips it on, as if riding it; doesn't notice
   it's not moving.)
Riding, riding.
Never felt freer. Riding my . . . comet.
Faster! Savage joy ticks my, tickles my
Itchy shoulder.
IT. WASN'T.—mother, water—WASN'T. EASY.

9. (Brief blackout restores opening scene of section 1, mirror uncracked and
   cocoon unhatched, but in reversed world: this time speaker is trousered
   American visitor, addressing voiceless toga'd reflection. Tree now hol-
   lowed.)
Stop stumbling; you might . . . wake up.
Round the round world I've come—how odd your togas seem—

To Tarsus. A salubrious clime.
But what makes borders blur between me and tree?
   (entering tree-hollow)
I wonder who's cocooning; glad it's not me.
   (Stretches elastic cocoon and wraps it around himself.)
My walls feel silky—delicious!—no, loathsome, loathsome.
IT. WASN'T.—drone-voice?—WON'T BE. EA—.
Closer than dryads to my splintry sliver,
Shrunk smaller than the grubs it's rotted with,
I hunch a horribly-sprouting shoulder
Deeper into the quilt of pith
To sleep 2,000 rings deep. . . . No, assassinate me
Out; skin me alive of the rind of forever;
I can't hold on; waker, flay me of deity.
(CURTAIN)
* * *
(Now entire monologue is repeated. But never quite the same each round;
not circle but spiral, time without end.)

TRANSITIONS

———◆———

The first transition (from timeless Zero to contemporary Part One) is spoken by father and you; the second by Dionysus-Bacchus.

Transition One

———————

(Addressing the offstage 'you,' the father-voice sounds like farce at first, then gradually sinister, and starts by parodying the preceding cycle's son-mono-logue: 'It wasn't easy being God/Compassion festered worse than thorns.')

(father: *The Monotheist Monotony*)
Fellows, it's not been easy being God;
The hohum festered worse than thorn or rod.

My cross?—ennui's insomnia.
And yours?—mors vincit omnia.

Virtue?—dowdy.
Vice?—frowzy.

You've stuffed with 'God' the sky that left you friendless,
You taxidermists of the empty Endless.

Such bowings to stuffings have weakened your spine.
Your only strong strength is your weakness for wine.

Whose vision is it, yours or mine, that garbles?
Men see marble, God sees marbles.

Oh and don't go bragging how far your spaceships flew.
It's less than the space between yourself and you.

You bleat, 'God doesn't answer me.'
Silence is still sky's wittiest repartee.

Earth?—call it hell's erogenous zone.
Creation?—Ask Onan, I was so alone.

  (you entering)
"I launch my brow at you."—Eggshell at rock of 'thou
Shalt not.' . . . But what's that shimmer from that brow?

"Lightning-prone even in dry skies,
Man's deserts have big eyes."

  (Exit father, turning his back on you. Staring after him forlornly, you
  regress to child-voice: *Game Called on Account of Darkness*)
"Once there was a friend.
He watched me from the sky.
Maybe he never lived at all.
Maybe too much friendship made him die.

"When the gang played cops-and-robbers in the alley,
It was my friend who told me which were which.
Now he doesn't tell me any more.
Which team am I playing for?

"My sci prof built a telescope
To show me journey's end.
I peeked and peeked for hours.
I couldn't find my friend.

"At Sunday school they said I breathe too much.
When I stop my breath cocooning under
Planks, they said I'd be his butterfly.
I wonder.

"Every time I stood upon a crossroads,
It made me mad to feel him watch me choose.

I'm glad there's no more spying while I play.
Still, I'm sad he went away."

   (you with tourist poster of father's stern Sistine Chapel face)
"This pin-up once (let there be light) lit up my Kinder-
Garten. I (he too) now crave new glow."
    (son entering)

       Shred him quick (or else he you) for tinder.
       Grow up and grow.

Transition Two

———◆———

Christianity was a Greek mystery religion . . . derived from the worship of Dionysus . . . the god who died, reborn Osiris.
                                                                    —Philip K. Dick

[Dionysus is] a drive towards unity, reaching beyond personality, the quotidian, society, reality, across the chasm of transitoriness: an impassioned and painful overflowing into darker, fuller, more buoyant states; an ecstatic affirmation of the totality of life as what remains constant— not less potent, not less ecstatic—throughout all fluctuation; . . . the eternal will for regeneration, fruitfulness, recurrence; the awareness that creation and destruction are inseparable.
                                          —notebook jotting of 1888 by Nietzsche

(Shape-shifting vineyard stranger of "Hacked" cycle returns, addressing silent you: *To Trigger Your Cycles*)

Will no one watch me? See, I'll dance on thread
Or hold my breath for cameras till I burst.
Step close, please; see, I'll pick your pockets first
And shine—like truth? like lies?—and then drop dead.
Word-juggler, shape-juggler, world-juggling god, and quack:
My names, unending as an almanac,
Spin round me in a manic spelling-bee.
I'm Dionysus (or a wino pretending to be);
Pan's one of my selves; on the Nile, Osiris another;

All word-jugglers; even my black-sheep brother in Galilee
Punned forth a church on a rock.[1]
But why did you staple him to a tree and sic
Saints on him? Saints made my brother
The killjoy he wasn't; they changed his wine back to water.
I'll stop all that, I'll make dead masts bloom vine.
Then, phobic of uplift, I'll hide beneath the sea.

*　*　*

The sea! What beast existences I'll wear.
I'll curl in lobes of shells and stall birth's war
For weeks—no, ages—in their womb-warm dark.
I'll urge obsession on; an eel, I'll swim
To every far Sargasso of my whim;
When I hear bathers laugh, I'll be a shark.
But who spiked my wine with empathy powder: what
Is man that I'm fool enough to be mindful of him?
Ah you, the born, have borne too much to bear:
At the edge you were always at.
　(scene suddenly shifting to Land's End)
Here's where you first poached air; just one step further
Toward poaching apples. Your beachhead on Now will falter
Till—raiding Then—you wrest from sky your future
Right here on Showdown Beach. It's where
I lit gene's hotfoot in your finny forebear,
Goading his panic[2] toward your future's niche,
Each world a globe of dew my cupped palms catch,
Each son in turn—from fin to claw to feather—
An outgrown father.

*　*　*

Savor the surf purr—how velvet my pillow of hover—
As I wait to be
　　　　　found: to trigger your cycles that follow,
My finder unaware he'll be a Founder
When he scoops my god-flotsam ashore.
A gale strums my vine-strings—it rakes my green hair in a furor
Of storm warnings. Change! I redouble my strum of your core.

Change course—new beach ahead—sails billowing fuller.
Molt creeds like crab shells, each 'virtue' a moldering fetter.
To make earth prance, I've been your gut-strings' fiddler;
Now fiddle your own; why remain—fiddle freer—
The 'what' you became? Become who you are.
No lodestar (though sky's Purest died to glow for you);
No road lore (no wise tourist-guide to chauffeur you
Or me through this most booby-trapped of planets).
But, but—what got my jigsaw puzzle mended:
What gets each winter's confetti of limbs unmangled?
O why was I fourteenfold scattered if not to decode for you
The Braille of heathen Easters[3] you abandoned?
Which, which of my shapes shall I this time gamble to goad you
You-ward at Land's End?

        *   *   *

A flame-scaled trout, I'll shimmer through your nets—
Like lies? like truth?—and gasp on bone-strewn sand.
Trailed fawning by lascivious lean-ribbed cats,
What child will scoop me up, what pudgy hand?

(Part Zero dissolves; man's cycles from "Waltz" to "Gods" now follow.)

PART ONE

The story of Newton's having seen the apple fall, has so captured the popular imagination that it has been quite forgotten that the fall of the whole human race, as well as the subsequent fall of Troy, also began with an apple.

—Hegel

Man stole the fruit, but I must climb the tree.
　　　　—the Son of Man in George Herbert's "The Sacrifice"

I would plant appletrees.
　　　　　　　　—Luther, on being asked what he would
　　　　do if he knew the world would end tomorrow

　　　. . . murder-shading trees
　　Are hair upon Hell's brow.
—Thomas Lovell Beddoes, from *Torrismond,* Act II, Scene ii

CYCLE FOUR:
Waltz

———

Must it be? Yes, it must!—Beethoven, 16th string quartet

Waltzing would be easier if we had three legs.—George Balanchine

And on the third day he shall rise again.—Mark, 10:34

1. (son, then you, pacing Gethsemane together: *Garden Hour*)
Toys don't know they're toys.
When they do, I ache.
Only one in twelve
Let me down. How pardon
Me whose 'Christians' broke
Twelve hundred thousand playthings
With loving fire and persuasive stake?
Unsaying all I said,
Locked out by God, I hang around, undead:
Gargoyle to every spire I ever built.
Around me children calling.
I cannot stop leaves falling.
I wear a rose called guilt.
"Wear pardon as a rose;
We too, we playthings too,
Make playthings wilt."

* * *

Toys don't know they're toys.
"When we do, we wake.
We rage, we rage at what we know."
That's half of one mistake.
I too, I tried to shake
My fist. Sky wouldn't quake.
No star fell out of step.
"Say yes then?" —Same mistake.
Accept acceptance so,
And still

        say no.

*   *   *

The hour in the garden,
The three days underground,
Changed me, made rage serene.
Remember all you felled
For heat or showman's sake?
The resin stuck around
After the logs were air
(As you will be) to make
The axe-hand smell of green.

I. (you, then father: *Road*)
"You up there, are you man's other
Eye, his third?" —Too blank.
As blinkless as . . . see that lizard?
See how he looks at that fly?
"Gods eat their sons."
Last Sunday you ate mine.

*   *   *

"Dew on tulips is—anyhow—beautiful."
Shut up and dance.
"Who blows the whistle on stars' tum-te-tum?"
The question, not the answer lies;
The traffic rhythm *is* the traffic cop.
"And you?"—The must of is.

"Slapslap of turnpikes, light-years of Milky Way:
Where to, where to? Alpha Centauri?"
West Newton. Somebody's got to keep the show on the road.

> 2. (you, then son: *Loam Hour*)
> *"Computing every tide,*
> *We calculate ebb and flow—*
> *And ask the dancers who dance us:*
> *Is it yes to the dance or no?"*
> Pressing clichés from roses,
> Plodding slush from snow,
> Best ask the loam that bore you:
> What's down beyond yes or no?
> *"You're not the only spark*
> *Went slumming down below.*
> *There's not an oak missed three days underground."*
> Earth is an eagle-launching cemetery.
> *"From plummets, summits; out of darkness, comets."*
> All mothers are dark.

*   *   *

"Houdini Easter lily,
Jack-in-the-box,
You'll rise next April;
Our coffin locks.
It's twice loam chills her sons:
Cast out, and at last stored cold."
Loam (you wrong her) warms your noon—
"Just once."

Once
       between exit and enter,
Between steps three and one,
You, the waltz's center,
Brush against sun.
"Globe-trotting Christmas tree,
Death-exempt tourist, be advised:
Hereabouts we're rationed on rebirth."

As man I fall. As God I rise
To fall still more.—*"Then Easter lies?"*
The crown lied, not the lilies, nor
The thorns.—*"Night twice is still the score;*
Noon once, and then where hide?"
Acorns whom April Eastered
Toward axe and ember and air,
When twice what bore you closes,
Go down clear-eyed.

*   *   *

"Computing every tide,
We calculate ebb and flow—
And ask the dancers who dance us
Is it yes to the dance or no?"
Drowning where skulls are and seeds are,
Down beyond ebb and flow,
Go down in loam's dense ocean
With an affirming no.

II. (you, then father: *Lizard Sports*)
"Waltz-of-the

> > *why-why-why:*

> > > > *born-two-three*

> > > > > *must-it-be?"*

Born-to-dust: Yes. It.
Must. On the eighth day I found out
The—er—dignity (the anyhow dignity)
Of a cosmos-job any grease monkey wouldn't be seen dead with:
It. Was. The. Blessings.
No irony intended—mildew blesses.
No tinted glasses—empty bellies bless.
No pollyanna—amputation parlors
Bless. As. A whole.
"And the parts, the parts?"
Tumors are odes to joy, every tapeworm a benediction,
Necessity is necessary—bless them all.
"Sure. As a whole. . . . As for
Parts, what does dignity—er—eat,

O necessary Tyrant-lizard Rex?"
Step 3 unrolls my lizard tongue for—
"This or that fly. But our globe as a whole is—"
A plumper fly.
"Toys have a—toys have a—Toys. Have. A.
Des-tin-y."
Hang-ing-its
          tongue-out-not
                 on-ly-for
Breath.

*   *   *

(father, then you: *Guest Night*. In this entr'acte, father plays obsequious host
of tourist resort; you play condescending guest with feather in cap. Stately
music from underground serves to exaggerate sardonically the singsong
rhyming.)
Guest night. High-stake games and . . . spending.
A birthday-party start; a breathless ending.

"On guest night, betting's not a sin."
You betcha life!—*"And what'll I win?"*

A box. Pay spring's Green Stamps as toll.
"Say, what's that digging?"—Not a mole.

"Is it to plant a flag, that hole,
Or for a folk dance round May's pole?"

More like December's cold North Pole.
Stroll three steps down to hug your goal.

"Umph, no big rush to get to bed.
That third step, why so red, so red?"

Red carpets guide your royal path,
As once to Agamemnon's bath.

"Who carved my name in stone above?
That second date—a 'date' with love?"

A hole you'll . . . come for. And a hug so numbing
You'll loll there till . . . the Second Coming.

"I'm a good egg, I'll close my eyes;
Now mix me up a real surprise."

'Une omelette-surprise' in a basement 'boîte.'
Good mixers fit so tight a spot.

"I smell a rose—what ditch that closes
Clasps me to be smelled by roses?"

You've nibbled a forbidden fruit;
Tonight you're nibbled by its root.

"Night thickens round me like a bowl,
And yet it's day. How almost droll!"

You booked 'a quiet room with shade,'
Well vacuumed by an earthy maid,

And here it waits.—*"Right on! Where is it?"*
We natives say, 'You just can't miss it.'

    3. (you, then son)
    "1-2-3, 1-2-3; waltz-is-still waltz-ing-me."
    On-ly-slots 1-and-3.
    "When we think we're free, our insides click
    Like perforated sheet music.
    We invented player pianos, but who plays . . . us?"
    The knowledge fruit's ambiguous.
    It's got two flavors, life and metal.
    "How tell'em apart?"—Steel cogs lack empathy.
    "Then the robot, not the devil, is the devil?"
    The devil was never the snake in the tree;
    He's the snake in computers named 'Apple.'
    "A narrow fellow programmed me
    With gene tapes, Xerox at the bone.[1]

The Eve fruit soured in my clutch
When in Professor Know-how's heart I heard
Cogs. Am I, too, a clockwork clone?"
You're each a sack of tick and turd—
Save when the selfsurpass of touch
Makes you linked circles.—*"But we're not.*
We're each piped in, one note's lone dot:
Gears in the Muzak of the spheres."
Ask Father Tapeworm which taped hole
Control can't quite control.

III. (you, then father)
"Oldest riddle, oldest riddle, we feel so much, we know so little
About how two can warm gate 2.
Inebriating appletree, give the woman thou gavest me²
The cider of forbidden myth: to share with me, to share me with."
In the day ye eat thereof—. —*"We'll be*
As gods, knowing good and evil." —Stop
Thief. Thou shalt not. Classified 'Top
Sacred.' From crabapple liquor
Lips pucker.

    4. (you, then son)
    "It dangled; she poached it from God.
    Her frailty's strength was my goad.
    Is its tang of the choices of evil or good
    Too heady now for my gut?"
    Bittersweet, thy name is applewood.

IV. (father, then you)
Then trust the Lord, your shepherd.—*"I'd sooner hug a leopard.*
When Jonathan Edwards said God was a charging lion,
I stopped opting for Zion."
When Job talks like Ogden Nash, let him first have the patience
To check (not 'lion' but 'tiger') his quotations.
"I can't believe in a flippant creator who talks
Half Genghiz Khan, half Groucho Marx.
God, show—am groping for a word—show some
Responsibility."—To whom?

* * *

(you phoning, then father: *Long Distance*)
"Clickclick. Connect me with father. What's the fee?"
The fee is you. Sir, please insert your dust.
"Can't I plunk coins in? Must-it-be?"
This is a recording: yes-it-must.

"Click. Information. Am locked in my room."
For Operator dial O in tomb.
"My heart clicks faster in the warmer O,
Tomb's hackneyed womb-rhyme."—What a way to go.

"Gods prowl both ooms (ask Lazarus, ask Mary)
Like plainclothes-men in airports."—Either quarry
(Ask Orpheus before and after) knows
My name is—
              "Eros?"
                        —Eros-Thanatos.

5. (son, then you: *Now that Holocaust and Crucifixion Are Cocktail
   Table Books*)
Waiting for dying? Tell me how
It feels to grow up mortal.—*"Ow."*
So long since I did dying on my own.
How do you manage it?—*"Alone."*
I mean, what does it feel like?—*"Cold."*
Resist! Young rebels, how do *they* end?—*"Old."*
But ethics—brothers all—. *"Like Cain."*
Asylums needed! —*"For the sane."*
Man's load, I'll share it. —*"No such luck."*
I sold for thirty—. *"Lambchops for a buck."*
From me they made Wafers. —*"From later Jews, soap."*
But Christians, being Christian, saved us. —*"Nope."*
But I'm Mr. Christian in person, not solely a Jew.
"Sure. By the way, Mr. Eichmann is looking for you."
Six million! Where can I find the memorial booth
For their lost golden dreams? —*"In a German gold tooth."*

Unique: I rose. —*"Some lambs escape the stew."*
At least my Stages went unshared by you:
I lugged a cross uphill once; say
If you have. —*"Nine-to-five each day."*
Who else blooms Easter back with April showers?
"All funeral parlors 'say it with flowers.' "
My parents didn't help. —*"Whose really do?"*
My lonely hour both copped out on. —*"Who?"*
My father wouldn't stop the spear. —*"Same here."*
O mother, I'd hoped it wouldn't hurt. —*"Me too."*

V. (father alone)
My sheep mask—so to speak, my son—
It—he—are they me or man?
If man, he'll cancel all I made him say.
But I've a cure—he can't bleat that away:
Time's. loom. can't. stop.
But if pairs guess what slows it up?
What if their second, their paired waltz-step
(Too tender for 'lust,' for 'spirit' too carnivore)
Is some fourth doorstep?
That pair, down there, ignoring me,
How dare—who made them anyhow?—gates are three:
Dumped, dunked, and done. Fourth cannot be.

(you interrupting, then father)
"Until. We'll fall until
We fail to fail."
Too frail.

(male you to curtain-shrouded feminine you)
"Too frail our fists to bash—or bless—
Deadpan sky.
The honorable daftness of a doomed caress
Our gauche reply.
Against the outer infinite, love weighs
Your small, lined face
And finds all space less heavy than your sigh

And time outlingered by our tenderness.
Quintillion worlds have burst and left no trace;
A murderous star aims straight at where we lie;
Our armor is: be armorless
                                        together.
Our shield: be naked
                        to each other.
Quick, let me touch your body as we die."

    (father, then you: *Dry As Dust*)
Not bodies; two dry-as-dust minds. Not touching; haranguing.
"Our flesh romp——." Mirage of brain's longing.
"No clasp outclasps two minds of parch,
Each the other's lush mirage,
Vicariously clinging."
Vicarious, vicarious;
The bodiless hugging the shadowless,
Hallucinating shared heavens from separate hells.
Two life-starved clever imbeciles:
Jailed in your own cerebral cells.
"Only from out those strict gray shells
Of dust-that-ponders can a bell's
Gold resonance come ringing."
Dust, can you ponder? —*"Till we do, we're not*
Circle but dot."
Brain guck peels off. —*"And song?"* —Must slough.
"What lasts?" —Skull's songless grinning.
"All, even anti-song, all's grist for singing."

    (male you to female you: *In Earth Who Wallows Like Its Borrowers*)
"My tryst with romany; black eyes and white
Teeth of the palest, blackest-haired of daughters.
Henna you prinked by Andalusian waters,
Dawdling—with scorn's grace—south of wrong and right.
O you
Laughed sun back hundredfold like caressed dew.

And did you, past my sonant fruit-tree strolling,
Hear hundred wines of air compel you back?

Then what a mist of longing our enfolding!—
Fused hoax of dew and wine, each other's lack.
O may
Coastlines of contour rise from mistiest spray.

No cosmic wrangles crowning either Prince,
Not all the stakes of soul for which They clash,
Are worth the angel of a lucky glance
That casual earthlings in their glittering flesh
O throw
At daily things—rain's tilt, or sheen of snow.

In earth who wallows like its borrowers?
What bodies can so sensuously press
As masks of unborn shadows? Fallowness
Can yearn the very sun loose from its course.
O would
That ghosts, through love, earned shape. If but we could.

I know you now; no romany your home.
Then know me too; no arcady my lair.
Formless you flash; I hope you, and you are.
Weightless I hover; need me, and I loom.
O we
Never were. Homeward to hell come flee."

*   *   *

6. (son, then you)
I'm back. —*"The leg of lamb that got away."*
My second coming says: unsay, unsay.
"This time—?" —No drugs to sell.
"No skiey trance?" —This time: loamy 'trans'.
"Transcendent soul?" —Transfigured soil;
Earthiness this time restored
To earth. —*"But afterlife—"* —Killeth.
"But healer, you'll heal us?" —Of healers.
They can't stop, they heal you to death.
. . . *"You once brought the Word."*
This time: only words.

The rhythm-words of a bell.
"Bell decodable?" —Livable, not knowable.
"Far knell?"—Try inner ear.
"Is your lamb bell this time a clown bell?"
Shh. Hear.

(Three-beat music, overstressed in jingly style, accompanies this
you-son dialogue: *Valse Macabre*)
"Are we waltzers or waltz?" —Both are trances;
All lambs are gray in the gloom.
"Are there dancers who freeze us to dance us?"
One two three, one two three, boom.
"Was the sky-climb the best step or worst step?"
You've lost both the light and the loam.
"All gateways feel warm at the first step."
The third is the same icy room.

* * *

"Can waltzes be ever a four-step?"
Can ever Antaeus touch loam?
"Can a door-to-a-door be a doorstep
Toward—what?" —Toward a tune, not a tome.
"Birth-yawn and earth-yawn are inkpots.
Who writes? Are we author or plume?"
A life is a Rorschach of ink blots
Between an oom and an oom.

* * *

"Are you WE first or HE first?" —Grope greenly;
There's a secret that slows up his loom.
Tenderly, briefly, 'obscenely,'
There's a step, there's a gulp outgulps doom.
"Why brief: Must-it-be? What bucolic
New romp waits up there where we'll zoom?"
Same meathook wherever WE frolic.
I bring you this news from the tomb.

(While saying 'WE,' son steps decisively from father-side of stage
to you-side. The music adds irregular quick fourth beats, despite
father's 'Fourth cannot be.')

CYCLE FIVE:
Bread

———————

Man lives by bread alone.
—from son's future new 'New Testament.'

Life is a place where it is forbidden to live.
—Marina Zvetayeva

Backdrop rises for bread sestets: gas lights, high hats, and such incongruous pairs as Queen Victoria chatting with Freud, Bishop Wilberforce with Darwin, Andrew Carnegie with Marx. Any backdrop will do if it connotes the liberation debates of the late nineteenth century.

1. (you, then son: *Green Mass*[1])
"Help us know deeper meanings."
Overmean is underknow.
Only skin is deep. —*"But symbolic skeleton?"*
O touch the touchable and let the symbols go.
"Bread of your mass was symbol." —Trust no carrion.
"Trust living bread?" —Man lives by bread alone.

"Black mass or white: which magic stalls the waltz?"
Black mass wallows, white mass wilts,
But green mass—. —*"Then can't I gulp Bacchic wine?"*
Not yet: too thinned today by love-in-the-head
Of pedant posing pagan. Get
Drunk on bread.

I. (father)
Come frisking you bread-drunk, you flesh-drunk,
Tossing your fleecy green locks.
Though I've lost my prodigal lamb-son
Who used to bellwether my flocks,
Come waltz to my chummy stockyard
Where a toy ends snug in a box.

(Enter white box on wheels, labeled "Your Good Humor Man," selling
black oblongs of ice-cream.)

(you, then father)
"What van each Christmas from the sky,
Persistent as an evergreen,
Brings ice-cream joys to sheepish boys?
Whose box rolls open like a grin?"
God's salesman, the Good Humor man,
Is landing on the village green.

"His van is white like what it vends
To toddlers frisking to the scene.
What tempting chocolate cuddles round
Vanilla from his snow machine?"
A ton of drippy black-on-white
Wee coffins drowns the village green.

2. (son, then you)
And I, who am half he, half you,
Whose leaves must redden to regreen,
I'm back—the patriarch's squealer son—
To warn of grins behind his grin.

Jump off Good Humor's limousine
Before white's blackness reddens green.

"Am I any less gray
When your mass is green?"
Is a pair no more
Than one plus one?
"Two tottering playthings can't rewrite the playwright."
Lean on each other; green mass is two who lean.

II. (father to you)
Spare me—you know I know you—the tenderness simper;
To stalk self-kidding lovebirds makes me purr.
You motionless nomad of your pleasure's pain
Through cities of the Calf and of the Plain[2]:—
College widow[3] of mirrors, even in twos alone,
The withering Narcissus ends as nun.

   (father alone)
Of all the ark's worst monsters, two by two,
The apple-biter almost bit me. Whew,
I should have sired some unsubversive zoo
Like minotaurs and swan eggs. What a jam!
All because Mary had
A little Lamb.

   (father to slaughterhouse tools)
Barbed wire of the nurseries of kine,
You five-line music-clef of grunt and whine,
Be lattice now for skyward paws to twine.
You dissection blades, act like garden spades.
Prongs that tortured, hoe my babes an orchard.
Sade, be Masoch; straitjacket, be cassock.

Steak grill, smell like incense-lighter;
Chef cap, bloat to bishop's mitre;
Veil your malice, be their trellis.
Look whose arms twine up already—

(you spellbound with outstretched arms:)
Trellis, daddy, hold me steady.
. . . Hold me tighter, hold me tighter."

*   *   *

"What happens to lambs in your meathook salon?"
They're swingers. But hang-ups have made them highstrung.
"Don't string me along. Are they happy there?"
They must be, they must be; they're dancing on air.
"We'll be chandeliers?" —When your leg-stumps clutch
The rollicking ceiling built by Butch.

    3. (son, then you)
    The meathook meat that got unhooked,
    I'm here to warn the green:
    I flubbed—trust only *vanitas;*
    Trust no caress that's not obscene.
    "What slows up sky's descending dish?"
    A sleepy fire from when you were a fish.

    The scissors-god has chained to a latrine
    Prometheus of a mutant gene,
    Who smuggled from the Pleistocene
    Such pelvic sparks that epicene
    Sheer envy turns amoebas green.
    "What spark can screen my dark from final dark?"

    Dark probing dark, face your own shieldlessness;
    From there retrace
    Your lungfish-trek from pop-eyed gawk
    To gash of face:
    Dragging your bleeding side on fraying fin
    Up mud-hill Golgothas of Pleistocene—

III. (father)
From jungle's green to fiercer village green.

    4. (you, then son)
    "I'm wilting—house me safe in glass."

Greenhouses aren't (weeds know better) green.
"Outside, how face the squalls I face?"
You can't defend, you can deface;
Go flick your semen at God's pokerface.
Hurl your own sea against the seas foreseen

By coupling on the village green.

Epilogue to Bread Cycle

[Backdrop changes from nineteenth century to late-twentieth-century décor: jet planes above, 'adult' bookstores below, and such juxtaposed pairs as Norman O. Brown chatting with Norman Vincent Peale, Wilhelm Reich with Anita Bryant, Allen Ginsberg with Lionel Trilling. Any background will do if it connotes anxiety about the new conformities imposed by the old long-achieved liberations. As if there had been no time-jump in-between, the epilogue resumes the preceding dialogue (which ended with son's: 'Go flick your semen at God's pokerface. / Hurl your own sea against the seas foreseen / By coupling on the village green.')]

1. (you, then son]
"We've deepened." —Every age its own veneer
Of 'depth.' —*"Your guilt-free fire left us freer."*
You've vogue'd it into red-paint placards. —*"We're
Passion's Paul Revere."* —Fashion's Christian Dior.
"Your bread-drunk pupils. Praise our plastered brawl."
A plaster Bacchus. Context is all.

*"Our milt does more than Miltown can
To justify man's ways to man*[4]
With the fleshpots the uptight fear."
Too programmed. So are spiritpots,
And both unlivable. —*"What's life?"* —A Wetback,
An illegal immigrant dry land turns back.

I. (father)
Sea, too, doesn't want you; you're riptide to tide.

2. (son, then you)
Rip, too, is tide; hands, too, are fins, only
Finnier, dipping
Deeper still . . . to handcarve deeps . . . until
Carved chaos forms strict form.
"I'm but a fluke . . . frayed fin, dud wing."
Of course. It takes freaks to build norm.

"My mutant seed may miss, plow barren shore."
Sick aims aim sure.
"Ah, the wound and the bow?"[5]—First, the village-green
Pandora. Dare it; open your
Self: sea's bratsiest gene.
"What's . . . who's . . . inside? And if all's fluke, who cares?"

   (son, suddenly exultantly)
Pick up the baggage lungfish lugged upstairs.

CYCLE SIX:

Rogue

The first and foremost danger encountered by organisms (which were all originally water-inhabiting) was not that of inundation but of desiccation. The raising of Mount Ararat out of the waters of the flood would thus be not only a deliverance, as told in the Bible, but at the same time the original catastrophe which may have only later on been recast from the standpoint of land-dwellers.
　　　　　　—Sandor Ferenczi, *Thalassa: A Theory of Genitality*

Seed spoiled by mutation.
　　　　　　—Definition of "rogue" in botanical dictionary

The origin of the larynx was to facilitate air breathing in fish. . . . The human embryo, when it is about five millimeters long, shows a slit in the pharyngeal floor much like that of the lungfish.
　　　　　　—Philip Lieberman, *The Biology and Evolution of Language*

The cycle starts when a parlor game gets out of hand, you becoming the lungfish ancestor whom you have been miming in a charade. This transitional "fish"—proto-lungs, four fin-legs—survived being beached by becoming the first air-breather, from whom all land life descended. The lungfish-you landed in the Devonian Period of the Paleozoic Era.

The speaker is you: mostly alone, occasionally in dialogue with father.

I. (you suddenly on Devonian strand, 400,000,000 B.C., addressing your
　　future selves of 1987)

"Where / when am I? I've left (behind? / ahead?)
You selves who'll now face twins you never had:
Twins younger than you (your own embryos)
Yet older (your ancestral dead).
You chose land's height? Undertows
Have long arms; hide.

Before there were veins, there was blood, not
Yet hot. Nor yet inside: tonight
Why is the surf so white and yet so red and yet so green?
Its quilt of algae tucks what shiverers in?
Before there was bone, there was marrow
Outside. Stealing shapes. How
Tight are you glued? A shape can be peeled from its skin.
Huddle in secret places, bolt that door;
Your twins—with half-dried seaweed round their faces
(A bit, not so you'd notice, goggly eyed)—
Right now crawl up your shore."

II. (lungfish you, lone in new landscape and facing the unknowns of sun's
   eye, hills, flowers, air: *First*)
"Just because I'm first of a newfangled race,
Is that why these eerie new props arose?
These sand storms: you call them a friendly caress?
This big scorching Eyeball: some predator's ruse?
It's rising, it's rising—behind shark-tooth rows
Of what? Unwet landwaves? The planet
An ambush? Yet this—a stemmed goldfish?—this beach-rose
Sways guileless; its casual fin-flicks erase
My wariness. Smells of growingness rouse
My snout with their . . . greenish flavor; they raise
My lungs to a . . . dry 'sea.' I plummet
Topsy-turvily upward and savor
The first whiff ever, ever sniffed. And vomit."

*   *   *

"Over the dryness, you empty white up there,
You're wreathing yourself with orange—where the Eye-rays

Stroke you. You. The . . . stuff I'll be breathing.
Me nobody strokes; moist smoothness, that's what I miss;
Blame the razor-runged ladder I'm on.
Ache is my echo since climbing rung-one,
A gagged echo straining for voice.
But vocal cords, still many an age upstream,
Will always lag behind their scream.
Why don't unbearables prod sky's deaf lid?
They can't. What's left is to plod very slowly uphill,
Each rogue with his backpack of hump to haul.
My feed, it isn't star song but raw squid;
The ignoring stars sprint on, at a speed with a lot of zeroes;
I live by inches—not by miles—of cosmos.
All I feel is the threat of small stones and the promise of moss."

III. (modern you to lungfish you)
"Here's homage, dear mirror image,
To the pilgrimage of our race:
From Argonaut to astronaut, from a puddle
On earth to a pebble in space."
    (father entering)
You're quite a couple.

               —*"My double."*
Each other's parody.
"Not soil, not sea."

          —Amphibious borderland,
On both sides orphaned.
"But . . . lung, thumb, brow. We shore-people,
We'll ripple tide." —You're but tide's ripple.

          *   *   *   *

    (lungfish, then father: *Jacta Alea Est*)
"I didn't want my double helix spliced
Into dodos, hippos, Al Capones, and Christ."
Your DNA dice. —*"Did I ask to be diced?"*
You're all rough drafts the Weltgeist
Discarded. —*"Rough on jugulars."* —Beneath
The die your landing cast,

Writhes all land's pain-to-be, from the gashed
Hare to the Lear on the heath.

* * *

(lungfish you to modern you: *Diatribe*)
"I should have been warned. Apocalypse
Shouldn't have made such historic (am I Columbus?)
Fuss. Landing gashed and frayed
Is not a Broadway tickertape parade.
Motorcycle gangs should have greeted me with whips
And lynch-the-mutant taunts.
Had even one sign said, 'Public beach, no lewd
Breathing allowed,'
I would have SOS'd my finny mother,
'Lungs not user-friendly, prodigal fish wants
Out.' Tell Dorothy's brother
That Nature does betray the hearts that love her.[1]
Dammit, I never asked to be a brow-evolver.
I 'is' a Nother[2]*; we Nothers—no freak from outer*
Space more freaked out. And if my quips
Are the desperate banter of sinking ships,
It's that my last self's fishing for my first.
The long fuse gets reversed; click—from my hips
Tick futures ramming fishhooks through my lips."

IV. (lungfish you, then father: *Chain Reactions*)
"No rockabye tide, no more of bubbly diving;
The end of glide, the start of wheeze and drying;
All this black dying, just to kick a gill
Uphill." —Swim back.
"I hear delirious welcome from my first beach,
A gull screech before the first of gulls is born."
Only some wind-blown horn.
"Is it land itself that clamors for life
Till birds arrive?" —Only the shells
A comber swells. —*"What glad*
Light on my landing pad?" —The brow infection
Called introspection. Its terricidal fuse

(Just one loose nerve) burns in you unawares.
"What cradle's now half rocking me upstairs,
Half locking me down?—snout aired, tail swimming still."
Race back downhill. —*"I'll bulge just one wee rung*
Toward brow, that super-lung." —Which then will blow
Up the show. —*"Earth's billion-year cradle, spun*
Empty around the sun?" —Let earth go weep
For what Niobe could not keep.

*   *   *

After the bang, the pyre.
"But after the fire, when sea
Shrinks into marsh, and marsh
Into desert, and all to ash,
Some overlooked puddle, not quite sterile, will then
Replay me."—And blow up again?

V. (replaying lungfish's very first glimpse of first Devonian strand;
    father, then you: *Ornery*)
The line where hills of sand end and hills of ocean pound,
Where tidal stride, foam-sandaled, turns around,
Here trickster horns of Land's End—wind-blown sound—
Lure you aground. —*"Am I never to trust?*
Must winds that hint, must wounds that sing
Bring traps?" —The fuse, the fuse! Rebound
Back to gullets and innocent laps.
"Rogue seed stays ornery."
On Showdown Strand they're stranded, the banned and the aban-
    doned;
It hurts worse to be land-bound than . . . drowned.
"Hurts us toward hardness and kindness. Till we—"
Feel drowsy, sink; feel drowsy, sink; feel yourself fondled by sea.
"I'm awake on the brink of a dune."
Spurned sea, though you sneak to deserts, hunts you down
As stowaway in your veins. —*"But that horn, that horn."*
Heed—drowsy, drowsier—sea's undertone.
"But shells, but shells, their undertow
Tugs shoreward."—Leave that siren tune

To stinking clams. One gallivant
On land, and all's undone.
"Or done. I'm gene's automaton,
Only I'm not. If brow—"
Can you guess whose out-of-time skeleton,
Stripped and hollowed, weathered and torn,
Was wind's horn all along?
"What's that to me? Can a gill, outworn, stall a lung?"
With your future extinct and your past outgrown,
The stripped beast is you, both your gill-fish bone
Of before and your loaded brow
Of tomorrow. —*"I dead or unborn?"*
You've lost. Go drown while you can.
"Too late. I'll—." —Don't! Sea loves you, wait wait wait.
"I'll always lose. Some losses . . . hone."
Halt, you're branded. —*"Stripped, I've landed.*
Make way for man."

CYCLE SEVEN:

Salt

———————————

Have salt in yourselves.
—the Son of Man in Mark, 9:50

The primitive eye-pits were open to the danger of becoming blocked by foreign particles lodging within them, shutting out the light. . . . One living creature, Nautilus, has an eye still more primitive—there is no lens, but a pin hole in its shell to form the image. The inside of the eye of Nautilus is washed by the sea in which it lives, while eyes with lenses are filled with specially manufactured fluids to replace the sea. Human tears are a re-creation of the primordial [Cambrian-age] ocean, which bathed the first eyes.
—R. L. Gregory, *Eye and Brain: The Psychology of Seeing*

In the human body, which is 96% liquid, . . . the kidneys maintain an internal environment remarkably similar to sea water.
—A. Anderson, *New York Times*, 1976

1. (son, then you)
Manfish, manfish, can't you see
Green barefoot, walking landward on the sea?
"I landed; why does salt still sting me so?"
Sea. Can't. Let. Go.

I. (father to you)
You stink—go home.
Sea is the stain sea's bath can't free you from.

2. (you, then son)
"Pillars of salt on shore,
Backward the glance we share,
Each melting waif."
You're each Lot's wife,
A tear that sheds a tear.

II. (father, then you: *Lacrimae Rerum*)
What lachrymose singsong must I overhear?
" *'Tears, idle tears . . . of some divine despair'*[1];
A trickle of benison for thirsty acres."
A treacle of Tennyson for nature fakers.
"Sweet wine (symbolic): from our music makers."
Eyewash (literal); sodium isn't sugar,
Nor are tears 'idle,' not since Cambrian years
First rinsed a proto-oyster's proto-eye.
You're still a Cambrian bathtub when you cry.
"Say, rather, we're shell echoes; built-in breakers
At every aperture
Still play the flutes we are."
Counting your holes, say (rather) you're saltshakers;
Your built-in brew is brine.
"But hero's trio, blood-sweat-tears?"[2] —They're no thirst slakers;
Dyed red or gold, your brine is still mere brine.
"Wait, we've a holier hue to anoint salt's wine;
Three spigots, one mine, two hers, dispense it: hers
Both slake a baby's mouth; mine slakes a fur's."
Are hers the rites of crib? Is yours
Sacre du bed-Spring?[3]
"Both sacred: a madonna and a wedding."
Slow down; getting tangled; just which color pours
From what of hers and what of yours?
"Listen, it's this way; there's milk, and there is milt,
And both white life-wines, reverently spilt, are—"
Mere whitewashed brine.

3. (son)
Landfish, landfish, try and see
Who plumbed the primal soup to scoop you free.

III. (father, then you: *Ad Astra Per Aspera*)
Though Lady Greensleeves yanked you from the drink,
You'll wheeze forever on the brink.
Land's End is what you flee to when you think
That it's Land's End you flee.
"I, soup's first wriggle, salt's Nativity,
Which am I: seaweed, sea god, or abortion?"
Plebeian algae, you're no Aphrodite;
I knew you when; fake me no pedigree.
Aghast at so embarrassing a birth,
Sea's fecund virgin Amniotic Sea[4]
Dumped—with a tidal peristaltic thud—
You. —*"Where to?"* —Upon some mud called 'earth.'
"To chin himself on mud is man's diversion."
And mud's. —*"When up enough to flaunt a bud,*
Both clutch what crowns a billion-year exertion:
One moment's green." —And then bog back in mud.

    4. (son, then you)
    Legfish, can you still not see
    Green barefoot, walking landward on the sea?
    "Far too far back an afterglow
    For memory. Too many skins ago."
    Flying browfish, cleave to her
    Who warms you—through brow's high thin air—
    As once through ocean's chill. Remember still?
    "Too many skins." —No numbers. Can't you feel
    Back, back where green's first footstep fell?
    "Yes, yes, her step feels beautiful;
    Out of a cesspool she churns forth a brain—"

IV. (father, then you)
A pickle pickled in its own urine brine.[5]
Out of that sty she—. —*"Now I feel her heels*
Goad the first frond from flabbergasted hills,
Whole fern groves now, condensing years to hours."
Condensing green to black, like book-pressed flowers,
Her fingers cram whole groves in one hot coal.
"On my scorched lids her gentle hand feels cool."

* * *

Whole ages end in ash an eyelid culls;
Whole cities—. —"*Cinders only my blink recalls.*
Dumps of a crematory that never cools,
My eyes are urns from which my skull recoils.
Oh sockets—sockets facing terribly in—
Can only her fingers face you out again
Before two staring graves
Flood me with landsick waves?"
You have to drown because you have to fly.

* * *

"*Reliving what my birdfish doubles do,*
Neck-deep in sludge and ego, sinking fast,
My bone-tree grabs for seagulls to the last."
Your brain cells, charging head-on against 'thou shalt,'
Spatter. —"*Salt, their gatherer,*
Revolves my cells in a briny ring
Through fin-paw-wing." —Through sea-land-air.
"*I, man, the whole show's consciousness—*"
The flow's, the flow's cracked looking-glass—
"*Am the milli-second of look when flow says oh.*"
You're here—no, there—no, fifty skins ago.
"*Because I keep on dying, I'm still not dead.*"

* * *

Because you're dead, your dust keeps flying:
You drink at dawn, you strew at noon,
At eve you're dried, at midnight strewn.
"*Not dust to dust the trek we tread,*
My lives and I; we race the rain-way home
From all my pores,
                    not dust but foam to foam.
Through drying selves my landlocked oceans knife:
The oldest through the youngest swim of life."
Through sewer-pipes your jailbird-puddles vault:
The wettest through the driest stench of salt.

5. (you, then son: *Sperm Pilgrimage*)
"Fish know of fishnets that have hairy ears;
Cilia are whispers only belly hears;
Am I still milt-bound by the billion years
That spill my fish in fisher's oldest weirs?"
When you spill seed on your most primal fears,
Out of a vein your grandma's grandpa leers.
"Then even from exile, exile exiles me."
You're owned. —*"My owner takes a bath in me."*

V. (you, then father)
"Cells recall start of all.
Ringed by spit—inside of it."
Now spit's in you. And flows and . . . ebbs.
"I'm feeling sick; my chest core throbs."
Tick.
"Rid of tide?" —Ask inside.
"Rid of gill?" —Gasping still.
"In shore we trust" —Dry up and bust.
"Why do all those buzzards flock?"
Tock.

* * *

"How long can salt hold out ashore?"
Years three score.
"But all things flow—look, every pore—"
What are six decades less or more?
"But veins flood"—six-times blood.
"But pulse pounds"—six rounds.
"But cornucopias of golden arc—"
They won't outlast their lamp-post in the park.
"But semen lasts"—two thimble-blasts.
"Snout's gorgeous drool"—two thimbles full.
"Nipples assuage."—Act your age.
"Sweat never stops."—Shore mops.
"We're being drained. For whose swill?"
Spill.

6. (son)

Statistics: every day somebody somewhere
Freely wills suicide by drowning in sea water.
    (you: *Sonnet On Man's Will*)
"You mad-dog foams of spray
(You'll never leap loose, tamed sea)
Gnash harmless at my knee.
My tech has harnessed spray
(The mech-stroking ergs you spray)
To slave for my engine spree,
While I sidestep elegantly
Your barking spray.

"Small numerals muzzle your immensity,
Dog-leashed to Law by meteorology.
Man's will, outstorming sea,
Alone romps free—
And lawless, law-giving, conquering, armed with the key
To all but itself, breaks daily in your spray."

VI. (you, then father: *The Delphic Gallows-Oak*)
"Is a man a bleeding throat of salt
Between a bed and a bed?"
The loan of white your father spurts
You'll pay in the end in red.
"What kidnapper has cooped us in
This garbage bag of leaky skin?
From ocean's cold we swarmed, we swarmed,
Red or white millions. Jailed now." —Warmed.
"Wee wigglers from beyond, cramped in a walking pond:
Bad plumbing sucked us up in pipes of blubber."
A vacuum cleaner across a salmon-run.
"What liberates red motes?" —The prank of slitting throats.
"And mites in white streams? Trigger me the slobber
Of gene-crammed swimmers." —Mass suicide is fun
When eggward fountains die in Thermopylae
('Hot Gates' in more than Greek): all heroes slain but one.
"Free both my life-saps to flow home to sea."

Patronize your local gallows-tree.[6]
"The stench of sagging fruit? Fruit's homeward ooze?"
It's always autumn in a hangman's noose.
"Can there be waters only fires quench?"
When hanged and hangman pair
Through the fierce wood they share,
It's three who mate. —*"And mix their brines*
Of white and red and oak-sap wines—"
Till shivering crab lice flee the cooling hair.
"Suppose in that hug-the-cosmos mood
A charismatic hangman wooed
All forests into gallows-wood,
Roping all necks in one all-draining drench?"
One universal spine-jerk would
Wrench free a global white-red-yellow flood.
"We'd hang like children's stockings on Christmas trees."
Eyes popping like a tourist gawk.
"Sockets reserved, old raven, for your beak."
But first you'll feel your big death squeeze
Your small death[7] from two bobbing knees.
I'll watch the dry turf dunk.
"Turf's oldest sprig from dead man's spunk,
An oak oracularly drunk:
Under its venerable trunk I see
What mystic rite?" —You woke
The planet's Delphic gallows-oak.
"Green nerve-ends rustle; boughs sway omnisciently;
All's hush." —Now oak root speaks:
'O Mensch! Gib acht! Man, free your mandrake-shrieks[8];
Hanging's your last Romantic Agony.[9]
When neck-twig creaks and rope-fruit leaks,
From homesick core you'll pour, you'll pour
One jailbreak, all at once.'
"As stockyard fans sniff meathook lambs,
You gallows buffs sniff each nuance—"
The wet-cheek tears, the wet-leg fears—
"Enough! My kamikaze penis rams

Wet fire. Skin's shattered flask
Scatters into wholeness. My lemming blood bursts husk
In spastic getaway from straitjacket shore.
. . . Then home again? Old ocean floor?"
Amazed to feel my heartless heart feel pity,
I've got to answer 'Nevermore.'

      7. (you, then son)
      "Down, all the time down.
      I had a penny, it went down.
      A toy got used to a toy, they both went down."
We're each a walking blood bank, overdrawn.
"Some toys can swim. Where to? Glubglub and down.
'All flows'—too fast all flows, all cheeks tilt down.
Sting slow, bless long, you sacraments of salt juice,
Cry slow, dear downward friends,
                kind wounds,
                         warm birth-sluice;

Holy-water of milk,
          good piss,
                   cry slower down.
All salt is red in the end, white is red, red is red;
To you, clown-lamb of the funny throat-line of red,
To you wet armpits pray when a tightrope goes down.
. . . Yet you—we're drowning—only you fall up."

Whichever tits you'll reach for, were my mother's.
Brother, we all—it's really so—are brothers,
Room-mates from the same nine-month waiting-room.
"You merely hitch-hiked in her." —Toward a hill.
"To zoom back up, on contract with De Mille.
Are you still ours
                or again your showman-father's?"
Drowner, I fell by choice into your downfall.
"And the end?"—I asked only for water.
It was not in the script of De Mille.
The bitterness in your stockyards

Is the bitters I drank on the hill.
"We didn't ask to be Christ's angostura.
You savor us safe above,
                    but the view from below—"
Listen—shh, listen—am I not glubbing too?

CYCLE EIGHT:
Bells

Half way down
Hangs one that gathers Samphire, dreadful trade!
                    —*King Lear*, act 4, scene 6

[Man's] final fantastic element . . . seems to consist of nothing but prov-
ing to himself that he is . . . not a push button.

                                        —Dostoyevsky

I. (you, then father)
"Down. Batten down our hearts. Storm over toyland.
We'll flee to deserts from the sea we are."
You swim in you, you'll still go glubbing down.

     1. (son, then you)
     Here up (warm tide compels)
     Here up is down.
     And down is down (compels
     Toward clay). Your Gulf Stream
     (You swim in you, I'm swimming in your swimming)
     Brings you red strength.
     Brings, takes; you have no inland.
     "We only through refraction see your diving."
     That's why gods shimmer. As through fishbowls darkly.
     "Why do harpooners smile at us
     The way wet mirrors frown?"

In father's dry aquarium of landfish
Some things are something else.

*   *   *

"Then I'm——." —Your shipwreck's
Own reef. There child-blood sobs against old coral
—*"I feel it sob"*—and shatters
On archipelagos—*"I feel it shatter"*—
Of sweetness sharper than sharks. Here warm is colder.
Who shares the cold?—*"I think I feel you sharing."*

II. (you, facing millions of years backward, then father)
"Eohippus, you I harness;
Fellow mutant, genes have borne us
Toward each other. Up your meadow
I outride my fish-gilled shadow
Through a forest-fire's furnace.
Ferns, compressed, turn black to stoke me;
Age-old coal turns red to power
What from fish-foam first awoke me,
Eating eons in an hour."

Landscapes, God's doodles. And their eraser still is
Fire. Demon colors: red eyes, blue hair, one
Wavy black fern, uncurling, uncurling its
Forest, back up from a coal, reviving, re-
versing time while a Pleistocene dragon whimpers.
Old
    jokes
        tick
            back:
My jobless jungles, nations
Piled up like wheels and doors, my jilted props.
"Headlights and camera lens can't cry. But living props—"
That pile—look twice—is just an auto junkyard,
Spare parts for build-a-man kits. Flesh
Isn't flesh, it's wired circuits. —*"Watch*
My electric overload burst free to the stars."

Funny little Prometheus, seeking fire and finding
Fires:
Blue hair, black tears, orange eyebrows—your newest
Rocket?
Come recognize your treacherous oldest
Fire-demon.
"My faithful fire-servant.
New suburbias from knowledge-tree's split atom."
You bit no apple, it bit you.

     2. (son, then you)
     Bells, down
     There, waiting.
     "Whose Morse code undersea?"
     If but you'd hear my signals as your own.
     "Were you that sea bell? Come swap tales of bells."
     Am in you not just when your lamb bells tinkle;
     When knife blades tickle, I'm around as tocsin.
     "HIS church bells soothe." —My cap and bells come jolting.
     Betray me when they bloat into a crown.

III. (father to you)
You'll gag in deserts on the brine you are.

     3. (son to you)
     Be with me when I clown my pain:
     Wounds are my offering;—take!
     Give me your shipwrecks;—how many times I've drowned
     As lifebuoy in your storms. When they swell denser,
     Waver, break,
     Allow the wistfulness of outstretched sound.
     Armfuls of arms-withheld,
     Eyes full of awe-dispelled;
     Knelled now by me.
     Sharing your cheated trance,
     I clasp your dissonance,
     Toss with your unkempt sea,
     But still
          clear-belled.

IV. (father to you)
Tide's tuning fork, rubbed sensuous on reefs:
Ask why what waits so close
                              pounds out of reach.

   4. (son, then you)
   Sullenness, you're my corrupt sweet worldling,
   Knowing (of seas, not sea) too much to be enough:
   Port open to all but the us of you and me.
   "Pouting against windowpanes,
   Sullen-lipped (like you, like you) with knowledge,
   I mock my idiot wisdom."
   Trust your wise idiocy,
   These clangs of 'we.' —*"Are they gongs of dead*
   Buffoons, still capering underground?
   Are they thorn-crowned bells on a bell-crowned head,
   Mocking a mocker's wound?"
   Allow drowned clowns to goggle from your veins.

V. (Exit father and son; inner dialogue in alternating couplets between your
   "wise idiocy," speaking in italics, and your mere "idiot wisdom," not in
   italics: *The Split Sea-Self*)
"Underground-rivers ripple.
Ripples are sometimes heard."
Child, don't hear them.
Sit down, tea is served.

"People get used to each other.
Sometimes this leads to harm."
Elsewhere. Here's a
Potful; cover it warm.

"Younger, were years more under?
Later, less haunted by blue?"
Patience; soon now
You will be deaf to them too.

"Once in a lifetime, buried
Rivers fountain and call."

Child, child, hear the
Daily kettle boil.

"Once; and who follows, touches
Sand? Or moon? Or—tell!"
Child, stop trembling.
Porcelain cups may spill.

"Children whom tides have altered
Live fierce and far. And drown?"
Quick, move nearer.
Tea is served, SIT DOWN.

*   *   *

(Backdrop sketch: sea with woman-faced moon reflected on it, face of
Botticelli Venus; brief far sound of bells. Long you-invocation: *To My*
Underwater Moon)
"Because you are the moon, I am the net.
'Who dares to dredge me?' asks your looking-glass.
Am not afraid to fall.

Cloud half your face in foam, refract in riptides—
You'll still buoy up my net for all your shyness.
(Beneath the waters warningly, Icarian corpses sprawl.)

Sun, matinée idol of matins, signs autographs of gold
On postcard dawns: 'For me the young men drown.'
Not I. They fly; I haul,—

Poaching for light. An outlaw, not a rebel.
Against the current, not against the tide.
Discord for stricter tune's sake, as waves are a moon chorale.

Your slivers of silver
Are sea's unshored rivers,
Shored in my veins' corral.

All spilt constellations—ask Lyra, ask Cygnus—I've fished them
For you. —'She's
Just left,' laugh the eddies of glint, 'on a broomstick of waterfall.'

I've trailed you from starlight to street light, the gamut from Alpha
To Omaha. —'She's
Off on a whirlpool,' they taunt, 'to a reef-guarded shoal.' "

* * *

"When fall-rains hone the cheekbones of my planet
And fall-mists breathe upon my windowpane,
How serene you are, harvest-moon bridesmaid! Till the deeps caterwaul:—

Then the rays, the rays, the moon-nipples ripen. Grapes of
Typhoon. For the drunken stallions of froth.
Ships know you then, barmaid of squall.

Every hundred years you bear one stillborn lamb. Then
Comets are humbler pilgrims; certain fields dream they are poppies;
The sore-throated volcanoes forget to bawl.

Now calm. Glass once more, are you nothing but bleary midnight's
Bifocals? Yet kennels of ripples cringe at the leash
Of your two hundred thousand mile call.

High low orb, oscillant atom as split as myself,
Act out our undulance:
Now my kite on strings of moonbeams, now my underwater mole.

Images . . . In the end what you are is the world's palest forehead,
Cryptic with wrinkles
Breakers scrawl."

* * *

"Sun, 'starring' as star, let her rattle her castanet of noons.
I stalk a murkier rondure, your silver-greenish gong.
I feel your pulse-bells toll.

Born not of sun but salt and moister darkness,
I shed the shimmer—need no wax, no wings,
Only the skin I'm landlocked in, cramped waves a moon tugged tall.

Before I trusted Down to buoy me Up,
Two musks—your sea lap and sun's halo—swayed me
Between a fall and a fall.

Then flaw chose flaw: my snuffable brief flicker
And your sea-moon's borrowed flame.
It took a reflected reflection to rekindle a burnt-out coal:—

Fellow cinder, more scorching than flawless auroras
Too vestaled to kindle and
Cool.

Once warmth cooled warmth to ash—the breakers rolled.
Then cold kindled cold to flame—the breakers rolled.
And still the breakers—I want you, moon—the breakers, the breakers roll."

*   *   *

"Then tide tugged tide,
My walled-in sea
Invoked your round sea-wall—

And waited long, and waited long.
Your rumpled mirror bobbed and dipped.
Are you spray's fluff or a sunk globe, too strewn or too chunky to fall?

Sea wilts our surf-buds every ebb,
Land downs us tomb by tomb;
My one poised peace—Free Fall.

Long the homesick sea in me
Invoked your sick sea-home,
But before the net can raise its fill, it must risk the lonely fall.

And waited long. 'Dive me-ward, moon,' my own ebb urged you long.
But now it's I who dive defiant
Cold curves like a ball.

I'm brine once more, I'm bounced from crest to crest.
No, I'm all net, and all my strands are glad.
. . . I've pulled the moon out of the water, it wasn't heavy at all."

5. (son voice offstage; bells again)
New Icarus is alive and well, only a little wet.

CYCLE NINE:
Stain

———

(ALL-SONG CYCLE)

L'amor che move il sole e l'altre stelle.
—Dante

*To be attached to the subdivision, to love the little platoon
we belong to . . .*
—Edmund Burke

I. (father, then you: *Pelvic Seesaw*)
That seesaw, chained to that latrine,
Stains love.
        —*"But then transfigures stain."*
Stain fades.
        —*"But first makes deserts green."*
I've a color-draining iceman, named Forever.
He's vain about the news that all is vain.

        I. (son, then you: *Landmarks*)
        Forever isn't here to stay.
        Only the local doesn't go away.
        "Well-scrubbed abstraction, thinking big,
        Tramples my local nest." —Some gritty twig
        Bounds back.
                —*"Creed's Rock of Ages—"*
                        —See

It split by unplanned weeds.
"Ecclesiastes said there's no rebound."
He's now the dust he warned of; vanity
Is still around.

II. (father)
Still babbling of green fields? What ill
Was ever cured by chlorophyll?
Warmth still runs down.

2. (son, then you: *Touchable Gods*)
The reaching out of warmth is never done.
Reach out, mix in, and weave a near-far other;
What's lost forever is what's daily won.
Give all—keep twining in—and get
A more-than-all: three dance a strict quartet.
"And pairs are threes (O Eros, unseen brother)."
And even a grape, so single in its glowing,
Twines with a twin (O winegod, flowing).

"What reaching up, though old, can still astound?"
Persephone is stirring underground,
Stretching up drowsily through melting snow.
"I see each calyx opening, row on row;
Whole hillsides now." —Her wakening flower-throat O
A planet's yawn.
"But winter?" —The warmth you spent is what you'll own.

III. (father, then you)
All still runs down.
"But gods—"
All. gods. were. immortal.

3. (you and then son in alternate stanzas:
    The Race Is Almost Meaningful)
"The day is opening like a fan.
The gold is dimming anyhow.
At first the gold looks infinite.

The cold erodes it anyhow.
Above our cliff, below our cliff
Two mirrors bounce back blue for blue.
The dialogue looks infinite
Till sky drinks up the wetter blue."

The shore that gets, the waves that give
Don't really seesaw endlessly.
Yet evenings loiter wistfully:—
World, world, what wreath from soil so thin?
The roots replenish till the time
They don't replenish. Many times
The warmth is gaining. All the time
The gain is losing anyhow.

"Have you heard it, have you heard—
'Just a little, just a little'—
Have you heard the tinkling sound?
Cascading down from leaf to leaf,
The freak is sun. The norm is waste.
We pay to see. The price is night.
Renewed in vain, renewed in vain,
The tinkling song of light's decline:
'Just a little, just a little,'
Cascading down from fall to fall,
In vain but paid for anyhow."

Though thinning down from world to world,
Yet rays can loiter wistfully.
It isn't much we hanker after,
Just a little, just a little
Resonance in so much waste.

"The day skims many little days
Like porpoises from wave to wave.
Again the peacock spreads its tail
Across the night. Till night spreads too.
One ray resounding—have you heard?—

Relieves all weight, renews leaf's clock.
Till running down outweighs them all.
Yet evenings loiter wistfully."

World, world, what tune for so much loss?
What makes your thin-soiled marshland skim
A hopeless rose from June to June?
What keeps feet running to your edge?
The race is almost meaningful;
The edge is ebbing anyhow.
Again, again the peacock tail.
The stars are cooling anyhow.

IV. (father)
Your race was never meaningful.
The loss is gaining anyhow.

4. (son, then you: *The Stain That Moves the Stars*)
Paired wishbones, to and fro:
Seesaw, seesaw can slow
Your cooling stars and days.
Then hours are numb and long ago,
And opening lips a laggard hourglass,
And living—dying—both an outworn phase.
Then slow, what lava, slow,
What stirrings, stirrings stoke
(Up from the core of flush
To the frontiers of gash)
A sigh so glad that space
Stays, outstays?
Slow the thick moment rushes—
Till time, time in reverse
Just for one stalling flash is
The last of the terrors, the insolent loveliness,
The stain that moves the sun and the other stars.
"The stalling lava stirs.
I feel swelled rivers stoke.
But after? Same terrain?"

As if flood hadn't been.
Acres of sandy plain:
Your riverlets fidget and choke.
The hourglass blots up the hours,
And in field and fire and skin
Entropy ticks again.

V. (you, then father)
"At least we seesawing lovers slow
Clock's overkill with undertow."
So Marjorie Daw rides again?
Then time lies low, hound knows his place?
Too tactful, arf, to paw at green embrace?
Just try it, try spring's growth—my autumn grin
Is 'hanging men and women for the wearing of the green.'[1]

   5. (you to son)
"Yes, too much ache in growth, even in fern and fir;
O to live before life was! I'd stick around stonier."
     (son, shrugging)
Then back to rockbottom, before all 'before.'
     (in reply, you solo: *Adamantine*)
" 'Animal, veg, or mineral' *was always the game—*
Tyrannosaurus rex kept score.
They fidget too much, the strivers, even the redwoods;
Faust was a bore.
Unlearning the two-foot and four-foot
And petal-foot lore,
I grew backward from quicksilver wisdoms—this morning
I entered ore."

"Pashas of quartz, hear my idolatries:
Gaunt jet at the fore,
And the squatness of onyx that Tamburlaine carved
For the Samarkand sepulcher,
And malachite's hawk-green scorning blink,
And coal's red roar,
And obsidian, milking from milk-white throats
Rubies of gore,

And turquoise so blue that the stone is *the hue*
And *'blue'* the metaphor,
And a certain stark flint so flinty the king
Of diamonds was slashed to the core,
And a tongue of stalactite a demon queen
Writhed for on eiderdown floor,
And that eye of the idol I can't pronounce
Whom the tribes I forget adore."

(son retort)
No eyeless ore, that invention of squishy flesh,
Till eyelids flash.
Branding leaf and life with symbol-making stare:
Man's signature.

(in counter-retort, song by you solo, with music:
More Wings than Wings Can Bear)[2]
"A leaf, a seagull falter.
What sudden warp is here?
Leaf, leaf on the water,
Gull, gull on the air:
Am I your core's decoder
Or all the globe's corroder?
Is even some age-old boulder
Outweighed by one brief stare?"
                        *   *   *
"Fadings on the water.
Driftings on the air.
The inward and the outer,
Will and atom blur,
Shaping a leaf-that-yellows
To Aprils without shadows—
And aimless wings to arrows
That never were."
                        *   *   *
"It's not just you who falter,
Gull . . . gliding . . . here;
It's more than leaf I alter
With meddling stare.

I, dust, am dust's remolder,
More height than stem can shoulder,
More weight than wings can bear.
Is brow earth's overload?
Do deepsea fish explode
On reaching air?"

* * *

"Fleck bob-bobbing on water.
Fluff . . . bouncing . . . on air.
Eyelash's flickering halter
Of gossamer
Tugs—and a whole world's shimmer
Obeys one lash's tremor,
Till sun, black sun, seems dimmer
Than inward flare."

* * *

"That symbol-making stare!
More weight than wings can bear.
More wing than wings can bear.
No shell can hold the meaning
That seeming gives to being.
Who is it thirsts while feeding?
The story of man is here.
Is here to fill and alter
The leaf, leaf on the water,
The seagull on the air."

* * *

(you, then son: *Alias*)
"Suppose we deep-freeze artifice
To punish it for being ice."—When it glows
Through, isn't this what's called form?
"Then suppose we shrine it (from outcast to cult isn't far)
By con-forming:

   Hail Tsar Norm!"
When official uni-form marches the muse,
She longs for the jester but belongs to the boss
And hides caps of bells under bays.[3]

"Then pariahs outsing messiahs?"—Pious
Soapboxers who deify us
Demonize. Distrust sky's bias.
Motto: in dust we trust.
"If life is dust's warm motion,
Death is—?" —Dust's chaos, frozen.
So's formalism's rigor mortis.
"But form that lives: what's its alias?"
Chaos,

       frozen doubly warm.

VI. (father, then you)
Want warmth? Jump in Aetna.
"Tamed Aetnas, flamed oceans—
The poet's, the poet's—
Launched bob-bobbing bottles."
Not life rafts.
"What floats is the names he
(The last Dionysian
Poet) gave to what sinks."
Images jumped to his tune
Only so long. When he died—

         *   *   *

   (long you-monologue about poet-archetype [unnamed: is he Roethke, is
   he Hölderlin, is he—?]: *Planted Poet, The Last Dionysian*)
"The night he died earth's images wrenched loose
To gloat in liberation at his door.
Now vengeful stone and tree-stump dare
To argue with his metaphor,
His workshops now but junkshops of dazed props.
Watch half-built skylarks rasp incredulous,
Finding no tongue to gain a song from loss.
Fixed-stars his fancy etched into the air
Snap back—now falling stars—to gouge his stare."
         *   *   *
"Words that begged favor at his court in vain,
Contagious jingles quarantined in port,

Send notes to certain exiled nouns
And mutter openly against his reign.
Senile young slogans in italic *gowns,*
Sojourners of Trend, tin tropes that fear
His metal-detector ear—all launch a Trojan
Pegasus,
         smuggling past the muse
A ticking bombast with a purple fuse.
While rouged clichés hang out red lights again,
Hoarse refugees report from Helicon Heights
That exclamation marks are running wild
And prowling halftruths carried off a child."

*   *   *

"But he—strewn bones, voice doubly strong—
Scatters with one strict tune
This mutinous anti-meter, the lumpishness of matter:
Glass shattered by what oscillating string?
Worm-deep-cold and deep-bass-warm,
Loam is now his cello, strung
With vine roots—listen to it drone
A dying denser than our own,
Rustling our lives like leaves.
Bell, book, and test tube can't uproot the spell
That's rumpling our sleep-selves free . . . but immuring them new
In holy blasphemous names. The selves fray through,
The names pulse on.
What's churning in our wrist's red swamp?
This trampoline spider[4] *thumping our web of veins,*
These two-way lanes of lung,
And the in and out that lovers tilt
Are but the spilt iambics of his song."

*   *   *

"Time was (too much statement too top-of-the-brain)
When his vox humana wasn't human,
His anti-abstractness too abstract, the satiric
Not yet enough heartsick,
Too shrill the engagé *fife.*
When worms scalped that brain-top of such thin 'relevance', resonance

Made him our tuner. To free ourselves back into silence,
We made him a halfgod, sealed in a soundproof shrine
All day.

      (Crouched all night like a land mine,
His skull-box's box-busting Jack-in-the-box
Is trapping us into his second, his bass-clef life.)"

         *   *   *

"He, too, is trapped; look who has risen
Sky-high from a wallow in foam.
It's the moon bitch—her tide-throb his prison;
What's fixed isn't stars but thrum.
The clock of thrum, the waltz on knives
We're each born barefoot for,
This terror and decorum all our lives:
Mere grace notes

                sloughed by her, by her,
Earth's orbiting ten-thousand-year
Tyrannic metronome.
. . . Scansion of flesh. He us: taTUM.
She him: wave's tuning fork, heart's hum.
She strokes (she, the orb with the mirror)—now paddypawed,
Now clawed—his forehead through coffinwood.
While he twangs (as lovers and torturers twang)
Our outspread pendulums of pang,
His own veins are land waves—the claw
Of the moon strums them raw.
Then noontide rays: sun's staring prong
Rakes moon's own tidal stare.
Scansion of scanners in endless chain:
Breakers must beach—again, again—
Even as rocks must bear.
Strung on that undulating rack, he shudders into song."

         *   *   *

"Stamp out all dyings headier than our own.
Oh no, the grapes we crush
Rebound in us as flush; on nerves of vine
We stomp in vain.
His stored up Junes make drunk our winter;

In vain we drive our stakes through such a haunter;
The seismic heart drones on.
Yet some sereneness in our rage has guessed
That we are being blessed and blessed and blessed
When least we know it and when coldest art
Seems hostile,

        useless,

             or apart.

Not worms, not worms in such a skull
But rhythms, rhythms writhe and sting and crawl.
He sings the seasons round from bud to snow.
And all things are because he named them so."

*   *   *

    (father, parodying "The Planted Poet," then you: *The Planted Clue*)
Beware of Queen Formcraft. Here's a clue:
Final drafts linger; her first drafts are . . . you.
"What happens to first ones?"—What's dumped in a bin?
"I'll stay in my . . . pad."—Where her feminine
And male rhymes openly commit
A couplet on your clean white . . . sheet.
"I can't wait to conjugate."—You'll be . . . declined.
You have a blank page's . . . page boy's . . . mind.
"I feel tense."—Your past is imperfect, your future
Conditional.—*"And my present?"*—Irregular.
"What part (of speech) am I booked to play?"
Each he and she is a sentence, a
Life sentence. Punctuated by dots of pain.
"But not—pain hones the final draft—in vain."
    (father voice changing from scorn to grudging awe:)
You're an O-cratered, dash-eroded plain,
Caesura'd with pelvic San Andreas temblors,
The meter that stains my sun and my other stars.

PART TWO

Stranger, you have reached a famous land, the abode of lovely horses; you have come face to face with white Kolonos—here in the green leaves the nightingale sings all day, here is the forest home of laughing Dionysos . . .

> —hymn to Attika in the Loeb translation of Sophokles

I am now of the opinion that our entire country is a great pack of wolves, snakes, and hares, which have suddenly been turned into people, and I've come to suspect everybody, and so we have to go on the principle that everyone is to be arrested.

> —ideologue of official love in Alexander Sukhovo-Kobylin's
> *Pictures of the Past*, 1869

> *The Gods of the earth and sea*
> *Sought through nature to find this Tree;*
> *But their search was all in vain:*
> *There grows one in the Human brain.*
> > —William Blake, *The Human Abstract*

Prologue

———————

I. (father)
When lives are green, not white or black,
And no affirms them more than yes,
When dots are circles staring back,
Never till then can heaven crack.

    1. (son)
    My father who stayed outside
    Still faces toyland satisfied.
    But what when one toy stares less blank than lizards?
    He'll wish he'd made man button-eyed.

II. (you, then father: *Folie à Deux?*)
"Admit you don't exist.
God, be an atheist."
Doubt me? I doubt you back;
It's man who's dead; left lone,
I sing duets of one.
"Duets of none: two dead-who-walk,
We're keening at each other's wake."
A case of folie-à-deux?—*"No, folie-à-Dieu."*
No, folie-adieu.

           *   *   *
    (you, then father: *Damnation, Definition Of*)
"I'm vacuum's wingbeat, you're its airless air."

Each fakes the other into being there.
"Are wings but what I wing to?"
What's creation?
"Then it's just me I sing to?"
What's damnation?

CYCLE TEN:

Pish

———————

Only two speakers: you and father.

I. (you: *I Want, I Want*)
"It could have been a planet fit for Eva,
There had been promises intense as noon;
And even what went wrong was almost right.
Our torrents, frayed by
Daily pebbles,
Almost reach ocean,
Drown in sand;

Yet dew still shines on certain lanes on certain mornings
That's neither air nor pool but waiting shyness.
There's haze, an orange
Gray that, dawn-struck,
Scatters like flamingos startled by a splash."

(father)
All man's flamingos are plastic,
Especially when they're not.

(you: *Truth Gibber*)
"When potter is hoaxer,
His marr'd pot is gibber:
I, clay-code's decoder.
When sober is stagger,
My foggy shines flasher.
Now mirror barks madder
And never is whether;
I, fever, am either,
My dot circling rounder."

II. (you, then father)
"Update me Seven Sacraments,
Improved for the now generation."
Father Pavlov's Consecration
Camp will—ring-a-ling—bring your nation
Salivation.
"You'll exorcize our Seven Sick-events?"
I'll exercise your Seven Excrements.
First, infant burpism. —*"Pat their behinds."*
Next, getting conformed. —*"A must for young minds."*
Third, breed and whine: Feast of the Euchred-Christ—*"at the Borgias."*
Fourth, laying on of hams—*"in holy ordures."*
Fifth, mater-money or mare-itch; that's holy dad-lock.
"Did you say: wholly deadlock?"
Sixth, pennants. A pollution for your sinks. —*"And then?"*
Extreme unctuousness earns you my meathook. Amen.

III. (you, then father)
"If we've no better fate than hooks to face,
Let's go down shooting, let jets rape space.
Man's your amok amoeba, mugger of the universe,
Ramming all Black Holes with our jet's white spurts.
I'm not afraid of God; God is afraid of me;
Watch me bully him. Grr."
Well roared. You make me shiver. Brr.
I mean haha: the roar's falsetto. Sir
Byron Pipsqueak a lone-wolf knight would be,
But the stance is too nineteenth century;
Outlaws can't titillate salons that know no laws.
"Fallen angels still can flutter dovecotes.
We'll hurtle earth loose from the stellar trellis."
Meteors no longer make fixed-stars jealous;
A comet sows tame oats.

IV. (you, then father: *Fellow Humanists*)
"My flesh creeps. Are you some black-mass Jack who Rips?"
Mistah Baal—he dead. So's any God of whips.
Now that all Squaresville peddles freakier trips,
What's theater-of-the-cruel and *humeur noire*
But Pollyanna's dildo?—'tis pity she's a bore.[1]
"Black mass—"—Was always white
Sheep in wolf's clothing. Night
(Better come quietly) has a harder core.
"What's wrong with sunny Truth that builds and betters?"
The windbag uplift of your capital letters.

* * *

Sun's thermostat, it won't be all that drops.
So many things must fall in day's brief day.
Stuffings and stilts; your heads perhaps;
At last the—
                    "Hands off sky! Let ceiling stay.
Nanny whom childhood counted on,
Cloud-capped nurse-brow of sky, where have you gone?
We wake up screaming now at the idea
That Mary Poppins turns into Medea,

Who turns into the bearded mutilator.
Give trust back, sky. Be roof again, not crater."
It seems I'm being prayed at; I
Am sky.
"How, sir, must we adore you?"—Kill.
"With hot heads?"—With cold steel.
"When steel blunts?"—Hands.
"When hands fray?"—Stumps of hands.
"We've used up gooks."—Try using friends.
"And when we're out of humans?"—Stone a rat.
Call it my kicks, I like my globes like that.
"They didn't say so in the Great Books course."
Ah, fellow humanists? Let's force
Men to be good.—*"But spill no blood, of course."*
Of course. —*"And no exceptions to that rule!*
Except to prove it."—You have been to school.
"And even if others spill some tiny bit
While we're not looking, we'll drink none of it."
Who talks of drinking? Just a sip.—*"A sample?"*
The better to rebut its bad example.
"Quick, hide it. Far away. It's not our thirst."
No, not at first.

V. (father)
Well then, sum up, O man,
La condition humaine.

  (you: *La Condition*)
"From skin-quilt's hell,
Hurt leaped toward heal—
And fell freezing between.
Who's run off with my skin?"

  (father, now in white medic jacket, brushing egg-filled
  hypodermic needle against patient's chest)
Kindly therapist gets you tranquil again
By planting something to . . . egg you on.
"Oh thank you. But what am I growing within?"

That tickling? Child, call it conscience's sting.
Inner growth tests your . . . guts; you must . . . shell out its price;
Else a great bug in prison lies.[2]

(father to stagehand angel)
He'll hatch his death's life-egg. It's a neat trick
To stick a wasp in a grub's meat.
A wasp and a moth feel alike inside
At first.
      (stagehand, genial chuckle)
      Till the wasp gets an appetite.

(father to you)
Wings are the stings you are pregnant with:
The tingle of grub becoming a beautiful moth.
"Wings, wings? Then flying to heaven is more than a myth?
I feel full of . . . life; oh I'm bursting with . . . health."

CYCLE ELEVEN:
Eyes

Why are Eyelids stord with arrows ready drawn?
—William Blake, *The Book of Thel*

Father you have made a
wistful monster;
Wondering stumps
and outstretched eyes.
—"you" in this cycle

Consciousness the Will informing, till It fashion all things fair!
—Thomas Hardy, *The Dynasts*

Re the sequential link between the next three cycles (Eyes, Book, Auschwitz):

At this turning-point, father's monopoly on creativity is being threatened by the awakening consciousness in the eyes of the toys he botched ("Next time I'll make man button-eyed"). To distract you, he dangles the bait of "spirit" ("book two," son's repudiated New Testament). The resultant Book cycle ends with this love-as-pure-spirit becoming so abstract and transcendent, so dehumanizingly ideological, as to give way to the unabstract hate of the subsequent Auschwitz cycle. The latter juxtaposes Richard Wagner's obsessive fantasy of "burning all Jews" with Nietzsche's lone warning that

Wagnerism would culminate in an anti-Semitic holocaust, a second crucifixion. Christ and this "mad" self-styled "anti-Christ" become half-brothers via
the changed insights of their *via dolorosa*.

I. (you to father, then father: *Paradise Lost*)
"Credo quia absurdum; *therefore, roar us—*
Preposterous tyrannosaurus—
The one sublime 'thou shalt': love's cosmic coo."
MEAT SHALL STUFF MEAT, whichever place you stash it.
"A pretty picnic. . . . What went wrong?"—An O
That feeds on feeding, not on food, a hollow
To film the universe, not swallow.
"Which hole?"—Not snouts, not bellies
But two frail camera jellies,
Outgaping lips and laps, unsatisfied
Till lids gulp sky. Would they were button-eyed!
"No creator willed what he created.
Why is it, of all the stuffers in your stew,
Only man mates eye to eye?"
No blank-eyed lizard ever wondered: 'who?'
"Where . . . when . . . was I injured?
Who . . . first . . . turned me inward?"
While thunder-saurians blankly murdered, blankly mated,
I, jealous father, scissored
Your lizard tail from your simian eye.
"Peccavi (Walter) pater, aesthete of ow,
Gourmet decapitator of mankine's terminal moo.
Yet there's a balance: you took my brawn, I grew
Elephantiasis of brow."

> 1. (son)
> Don't call it paradise regained.
> Not till halved selves are joined.

II. (father, then you)
A bulge will bulge, whatever place you stash it,

A forehead bump avenging a lizard stump.
Man was a—man was a—Man. Was. A.
                                        lizard,
With tongue and tail outstretching,
But he flicked for flies too high;
His eye shook sky.
So I cut each swaggering staff off
And (for laughs) remembrance half off,
Lizard tongue and tail still twitching
With the frenzy of a toe
Felt in gangrenes amputated
Half a million years ago.
"What creation asked to be created?
Blank-faced to us all, what have you done?
Father, you have made a
                        wistful monster:
Wondering stumps
                and outstretched eyes."
And every newborn child still (haha) cries.

            2. (son, then you: *Lids*)
            Image of ambush,
            Hushingly dim:
            Gold-bellied hornet
            Hanging from ceiling.
            Torment is dangling
            Feelers at man.
            Antennae are trailing from
            Gold chandelier;
            Fearing no ambush,
            Home come the children,
            Bearing a dutiful
            Image of sky.
            Holding a teddy bear,
            Children are sleeping,
            Famished by scrimmage,
            Depressingly old.
            Image of ambush,

Noise on the ceiling:
Hum that accuses
Hangs from the sky.
Seeping caressingly,
Gold of the ambush
Oozes on sleepers
Beautiful poison,
Sky's ancient fangs.

*   *   *

"Eternity was blank.
Anchorless was sea.
Eye, catalyst I,
Gaped once—and all reshaped."
Blaze it to urb and orb:[1]
Lids etched a human gaze.
"Poking the dinosaur blankness of Will
Till numb toys woke."
Orbitless wonder broke loose,
Noosing the stars in its curve.
"Stamping my brand on each you."
Universe squeezed by that clamp
Into a human-scale thin
Nerve-end of lids.
"Inward reversal of lids
Made what I never planned,
Peeping too deep into core.
Lids, give me back my sleep."
Spanned by such finite lids, what infinite gizzard!
"More span than lids can bear.
Tear off, tear off my lids.
Blurt it, what can't be hid:
Rid me of me—it hurts."
Lizard, lizard, fade.
Man has invented man.

III. (father)
Yoking the light-years to an eyelid's span,
Man ogles cosmos—cosmos boggles at man—

3. (son)
Boggles when stares of stockyard steers—
Up from their Shepherd's butcher stores—
Indict his hook of stars.

IV. (father, then you: *"Crossing the Bar"*)
That meathook, it's effective
For meat's insurrective gaze;
When heels tread ceilings, blink goes blank.
Slow-motion backward backward, the eyeball's camera slips:
You'll dribble (like a leaky image bank)
A lifetime's movies. As the. Lifeblood. Drips.
"At least 'I'll see my Pilot face to face.' "[2]
Not face to face but face to heel: your hook perspective
Will see. Your pilot. Caper. Upside down.

* * *

"Dad the showman, son the clown:
Odd god team—how did you begin it?"
As oldtime-gaslight stage magicians,
Cadging—from yokels—shabby souls,
Then trudging through rain to the next fleeceable planet.
"That's all? No headier miracles from omniscience
Than juggling atom's bubble balls?"
Just this: our sleights of hand in music halls
(Worlds out of hats, dolls out of genes and glue)
End up (we more surprised than you)
True.
"Then how can I see reality's real look?"
Stand on firm air, suspended from meat's hook,
And choose your god, he Masoch or me Sade,
Two mirror-image stars, in orbit whirled.
"Two thoughts cavorting in the skull of space,
Bouncing earth back and forth on rival rays."
Seals catching your very inflated rubber world.
"Not rubber. If hooks prick us, don't we bleed?"[3]
Bleed what? Sawdust? Things don't know they're things.
"Do gods?"—Yes. No. Well, once. At christen-ings
Of eyes, of first eye-open-ings.

4. (son, then you)
An apple's glint woke eye cores up.
Since then, God dreads the light they cup.

V. (you, inventing long fantasy-folktale, then father)
"Ritual of the opening eye;
Midwives, elders standing by;
Whirlwind suddenly from high.
Patriarchs in hoarse outcry:
'Whom have we forgot to call?
Mirror, mirror on the wall,
Who's the most jealous god of all?'
Gaunter than a demon king,
Who stomps into the cradle ring?
His beard trails incense like a censer
But spiced with something oddly denser.
Holy water? Sulphur? We sniff tenser:
What's this, who's scorching cradles?—it's his glower.
Our hair-ends rise; we grovel lower
And flatter height:—
Pasha supreme of all that's man's
(Except for cradle's opening glance),
Bull-charge of Nineveh, jihad of Fez,
Babe-muncher of the Punic furnaces,
War elephant of Punt with tusks so bright
They're double-sunrise when you gore the night:
While peacocks preen on skull-bricked terraces,
You gorge your crows on breasts of princesses,
Tableau vivant of black on white.
The lard of khans anoints in curls
The Assyrian beard[4] your tantrum-toss unfurls—
No, we mean the beard your beautiful rage unfurls,
Scattering moths—we mean myths.
But why you're here at eye-open-ings
Is still unclear."
Like legend's uninvited witch,
I've come to curse the newborn niche
Of sky's arch-foe.—*"Who's that?"*—Two oyster wings.

5. (you, then son)
"What flies at lord with oyster wings?"
Eye shells rise, eye pearl stings.
"Lids fear lord's spells."—Against lid's light
No spells blast right.

VI. (father, beaming benevolently at angel of death and handing him coins)
My pet mortician, he'll blot out that blight,
He'll seal those wobbly Jello jars of sight;
His penny ('for your thoughts')[5] will weigh down tight
Lid's light.
    (father solo)
I'd thought only horses need blinkers; I wasn't thinking of thinkers.
I overlooked eye's look and thought it a spoof
(The infallible always goof) when marrows shook
Forth arrows.

6. (you, then son)
"Against his hex, what word protects?"
Your pulse-bells: wistful, wistful.
"I've felt it, how you meant it when you hinted,
'Allow the wistfulness of outstretched sound.' "

VII. (father to angel stagehands)
In the beginning was the word, but it got unbound:
Ear's link with eye—I keep forgetting it—rhyming
Not quite with . . . 'zestful'? . . . 'blissful'?
Some lamb word . . . listen . . . echoing:
Allow the—yes, of outstretched sound allow—
What allow? 'Wilful'? 'Misty'? Shove me a
                                          fistful
Of clay to build them a Trojan dove, a new sort of
Testament luring eyes too . . . wish-ful.
    (stagehand angels in consternation)
Omnipotence, where are your big guns now?
    (father raving)
My fit comes when young lids—I'm falling, stop,
They yank me down—what have I done?—

A thing's become an unthing monster—
Book two, distract them in or up
With soupy love, to hide my butcher hook;
Divert them to my camouflaged stockyard arch.
Not flesh—no, dangle an inedible spinster
Named 'Spirit.' To the meatworks forward march.
 (Darkness; angel band strikes up wordless strains of 'Onward, Christian
 Soldiers'; strains continue, but fainter, through opening lines of BOOK
 cycle that now follows.)

CYCLE TWELVE:

Book

———————

Plenty of hope—for God. . . . Only not for us.
—letter of Kafka

Thou hast conquered, O pale Galilean.
—A. C. Swinburne's version of
Emperor Julian's "Vicisti Galilaee," 363 A.D.

"A constant appearance of frivolity *is the correct mask for stoic hardness
toward one's self."*
—from Nietzsche's letter of July 23, 1885,
to Heinrich Köselitz

———————————————————————————

Speakers: father and two archangel flunkies, launching a book against an
awakening. No you voice; occasional interjections from unseen son. Setting
(as in cycle three): new California yet old Galilee.

———————————————————————————

I. (father, echoing his last appeal of EYES cycle:)
That was a close one. Our strategy conference—look,
The apes are waking—convenes. Yes, bait my hook;
Launch hate-of-earth as love-of-spirit.
But one front's crumbling fast—repair it:
My first-born sss—don't name him—having quit,
Who'll play his book?
    (Gabriel)

Can't trust your you-know-who, he's on the lam;
But if YOU—no, I'm being indiscreet—
  (father)
I get it; disguise me as his book-two lamb.
But can't I thunder just once? It's such a treat.
  (Gabriel)
You'd startle your quarry; script says bleat.
  (Gabriel whispering to Michael)
Quote him the beast-with-poor-posture[1] bit.
  (Michael to father)
Slouch on, rough beast, towards Disneyland to be born.
The city of us—'The Angels'—is savior-prone.
  (father shuddering)
Not that! Must I really? Has it got to be L.A.?
  (Michael firmly)
No choice; where else is tomorrow today?
And yesterday: say, around . . . I A.D.
  (Gabriel to father more tactfully)
To foil a sss—saboteur, could a . . . a dad this time play
(Am just thinking aloud) Galilee?
  (father shrugging resignedly)
Then no more patriarch macho; Gabriel, Michael,
Trigger the soft-sell milksop cycle.
Stow my long beard in mothballs, paint me paler;
Float me in flowing gauze, ethereal tailor.
  (father, bossy-voiced, to pinpoint's infinite cluster of stagehand angels)
Can't I turn my back but you're at it again,
That group tingle on that snug pin?
Go fetch—on the hop—scene and prop.
Cast: Sunbelt America. Time: late Rome.

  (Gabriel recites his book-two scenario: *Slouching Messiahs*)
Messiah weather! And here they come,
Shlemiels in sackcloth, not Hellenic
But from some Hellenistic clinic,
Declaiming as God's misty love
The gorgeous mush Greek strictness gypped us of.
At once from the woodwork where book two was lurking,

Each soulful creep comes levitating:
The western deep thinker in mystic-east drag,
The Abominable Showman of confess-it-all brag,
Breast-beating jailbirds of moral-jock sermons,
Saved Magdalens brandishing born-again hymens.
  (father applauding merrily)
Healers, healers, exorcizing sanity.
Humanitarians, lynching humanity.

    1. (offstage son, unseen this cycle: *The Gospels*)
    Four tone-deaf reporters gave as gospel what
    They thought they got.

II. (Gabriel)
Shrinks now vend mantras to pioneers' grandsons.

    2. (son)
    In my father's house are many Mansons.

III. (Gabriel)
Three bumbling kinglets, straight from Ruritania,
Confusing stars of sky and of big brass,
End up in Bethlehem Steelworks, Pennsylvania,
And strew God's myrrh on napalm, nuke, and gas.
  (Michael)
Don't leave out ascetics in hairshirts (lined with mink),
Heart's haemophiliacs (bleeding red ink).

    3. (son)
    No pestilence, not even progress, so wallows in blood
    As leader-prone Milquetoasts that long to do good.
    When earth's foundation lurches,
    Who'll tell these carnivorous sheep
    That only clowns build wise churches
    And only clear waters are deep?
    Doubt poisons invalids, doubt strengthens fierce
    Laughers with Attic salt in their tears.

What's blocking doomsday's trendy tread?
A bookshelf called classics in a language called dead.

IV. (Gabriel)
Ever since 1 A.D., when Pan paid his obol
To Charon,[2] Greek gods have been downwardly mobile.
    (Now Michael recites his own book-two version, *Doomsday-Cocoon USA*,
    broadening the locale:)
Thou hast conquered, O tanned Californian[3];
Your freeways that once were dune
Are nylon threads of an immense cocoon.
Inside the berserk plastic of that dome
A god-moth stretches mutant wings. Stoned Rome,
Deaf to the Geigers beeping,
Shares—in Last Suppers at Ashbury and Haight—
The burgher communion of holy self-hate:
A gorged consumer's burping.
    (Gabriel)
While they're crooking the pinkie of their clenched fist,
What's haunting Carmel, Cal, or is it
Rome's Carmel legion in Bible Land?
Nix on chronolgy when time's a rubber band.
    (Michael resuming his *Doomsday* scenario)
Snappo! Hear Pilate's sentry try to bind—
'Halt, who haunts there?'—spooks, or is it wind?
'This outpost,' he gripes, 'is a wound
Draining us eastward; by Isis, I'll bar
Un-Roman cults. Are you Attis or
Jim Jones? Well, what's one more
God, way out here beyond the *Limēs?* I fear
I'm going native.' Instead of aiming spear
Or laser and shouting, 'DANGER! Saviors are
Loose,' the centurion wavers: 'Beg pardon, ghostly sir,
What's a poor soldier far from home
To make of . . . whom?'
Centurion Humphrey Bogart, gone solemn about yogurt,
Gone soupy about Buddhas, stops whistling at bermudas,

Goes squish at core.
(And all the while the Goths are at the door.)
Shacking up with nothing warmer than a name—'mankind,'
Feeling guilt for not being lame—or halt or blind,
Watching the green go brown (where they say Pan left town),
He joins the Forum sit-in for pulling out of Britain
And kneels where once he nailed . . . while an empire reels.

(father)
WORLD'S END, while . . . with drive-in dryads endowed by zen tycoons,
Sandaled druids hoard body-fluids and get intense about prunes.

4. (son)
This time let the cup from sky
Pass me by.
Let Mithra this time or Cybelē
Try my tree.
What's this, what Star-tipped crest flies home
To Bethlehem?
The only flying apple-tree
Is stalking me.
Oh not again? Oh can't I sleep
Like any non-immortal sheep?
Grant applewood, oh this time, what it lacks:
Axe.

V. (father)
My cart of strolling players is bouncing down
A pot-holed road on a run-down planet's run.
With meathook masked as shepherd's crook
(Father as son, the Nicene two-as-one)[4]
I'll mount a sermon, quaint with pastoral isms.
Full speed ahead, and damn the anachronisms.

5. (son)
Full-throated Homer never swerves;
Old Yahveh's book is beautiful and strong;

The script I'm nailed to is anemia's song,
A late-Rome mishmash for weak nerves.

VI. (father to angel bouncers armed with truncheons)
Wearing sheep's clothing in my paleface book
Saved me from getting hooked on my own hook.
Now save me from has-been gods from the wrong hill[5]
Who heckle his . . . my . . . Mountain Sermon.
Here's a chance, Christian envy, to pelt Olympus with swill:
Here's EROS—tickle him with vermin;
LAW—for woozy Spirit to determine;
TRADITION—skin him of his ermine;
MUSES—abort them with a dogma pill;
PAN—make him useful as a goatskin rug;
Aretē—switch to 'ugh.'
. . . They're laughing. Not at me? At *me?* You're sure?
Dark angel, roast them on my lower floor.
'Truth'?—bash him to my shape with moral truncheons.
'Pride'?—break him, break him—harder—with bad conscience.
'Irony'?—against that sneak I've no defense.
. . . Quick—intercept two god-spies at the passes
Before they slip to Nazareth from Parnassus
(Their real names Aphrodite, Dionysus);
They've false credentials reading 'Bread' and 'Wine';
Paul, Paul, degrade them into Breed and Whine.
Don't kill them—drive them underground, call them 'vice,'
The lions thrown to the Christians, the cats crucified by the mice.
Did tramp-god riffraff think they pulled me under?
Well, foxy grandpa cackles in his thunder
(Just slightly senile and again divine):
'Mirror, mirror on the wall,
Who's now the fairest god of all?'

6. (son)
Time-travel's only torture rack,
By magnet tugged, is circling back.
Can I dodge its flying tree?
Suppose the magnet tug is me?

VII. (father to silent you, who has been eavesdropping in back)
Before you sow some pagan oat
Or rummage in some Attic attic,
Bear with an old man's dirty gloat:
The dance of Aphrodite creaks arthritic—
How short the touch-god's flowering!
Earthman, from her Arcady returning,
Knowing April muffed beyond recall,
Try my abstracter grove; for the discerning
My greenless garden sprouts in fall.
Then fungi—then my pure white parasitic
Ideologies—sprout lushly tall.

      7. (son to you)
      Between two parks, you're tottering on the wall.

VIII. (father to you)
Come jump into the fairest park of all.
Fall's crisp credos, dogmas churning,
Cheery smell of witches burning.
Jellyfishes, pink with yearning,
Clasp as bone the rock of faith, and screech
These loving anathemas the Gospels preach:
Damn 'ye who mock me'—crime of thinking neat;
Damn 'things of this world'—crime of tasting sweet;
Damn 'scribes'—for passing ancient knowledge on;
Damn 'Pharisees'—for sticking to book one;
Damn 'publicans'—oh, that's enough damnations.
Call my damn hate-feast 'brotherhood of nations.'

CYCLE THIRTEEN:

Auschwitz

Richard Wagner makes a drastic joke to the effect that all Jews should be burned at a performance of Nathan the Wise.
　　　　　　　—Frau Cosima Wagner's diary note of
　　　　　　1881 about a theater fire killing 400 Jews; cf.
　Hagen's drastic jokes in the Nibelung epic of 1200.

Whoever wants to understand National Socialist Germany must know Wagner.
　　　　　　　—Hitler at the Wagner festival in Bayreuth

Remain faithful to the earth . . . That Hebrew whom the death-cults honor, he died too soon. . . . Perhaps he would have learned to love the earth and also to laugh . . . He would have recanted his own doctrine . . . He was noble enough for that.
　　　　　　　—Nietzsche, *Thus Spake Zarathustra,* 1883–1885,
　　　review of New Testament, predicting Christ's recanting

The hate spell that just ended the BOOK cycle gets dispelled by the song ending this new cycle: the Jewish Son of Man confronting the death camp. Until then, you and son argue about son's unnamed adopted brother, Nietzsche, the one philosopher who warned against a "future slaughter of Jews" by a "Wagnerite dictator." Nietzsche went mad in 1889, year of Hitler's birth in Braunau.

Hypothesis for this cycle: into a vision of "burning all Jews" at the *Nathan* play (Lessing's Age of Reason plea for tolerance), Wagner was projecting—being unsure of his own "Aryanism"—a rather different fire-image, that of the fire-trapped Germanic Hagen. The mass-murderer Hagen perishes only after wiping out all the "non-Aryan" Huns in the flaming "holocaust" ending the Nibelung epic, whose hexameters Richard and Cosima had been reading. Hagen's "tread down the flames in blood" is a direct quote from section 35 of this medieval epic.

---

1. (son, then you: *Twilight of the Idols*)
Later, my secret brother—he foresaw
A new, a death-camp Golgotha.
"Your brother?"—Born posthumous: here in my new
New Testament.—*"His mind blew up his skull—"*
The day his cup (he, too, swigged gall) was full.
"And his Contra Wagner *ravings?"*—Decode them; they warn
Of my Jewish death, and dead demons about to be born.
"Neo-Nibelung demons beyond good and evil?"—No.
Below.
The Birth of Travesty from the Spirit of Bayreuth.[1]—*"Chant
Their twilight the way the earlier epic scanned."*
Trapped in his Führer bunker, the Nibelung Hagen said—
(She and dear Richard scanning those six-beat rhymes in bed)—
Said,
         'Tread down the flames in blood.'
                                 —*"Six million bled."*

2. (son, then you: *Human, All-Too-Human*)
Their blood changed my Christian other-cheek love to lies.
"And now you forsake the sky that forsook you twice?"
It's what my brother predicted in the bad review
He gave book two.
*"Absurd your both being
                    parsons' sons,
And he in Bartlett's Quotes for having once
Said God is dead."*
Yet heaven-storming when he anti-baptized
His . . . my . . . nailed self by becoming The Anti-Christ.
"Thus spake schizo. And don't leave out failed megalo."

Nor jailed Dionysus. Ecce Homo.
"Bat swarms of masks-within-mask veiled his hubris."
All that. Yet when—from his abyss—he sailed
Skywards his skiff of words,
It was mind's lonesomest saga. —*"Don't leave out syph—"*
In 1889 sky's panic poxed him gaga.

3. (you, then son: *A Scholarly History of German Romanticism*)
"Though cosy sister-hand
Offered him exile's end,
Still he roamed glaciers for
Lost Ariadne's spoor;
Spurned as a yoke
Folk-bard's amenities, pipes puffing meerschaum peace."
Volk-bard's Eumenides, pipes flushing beer-foam piss.
"You're Kulturbolshevizing. Don't knock any moral majority."
How gross of me. Is that why Eichmann's
Kultur cleaned me up with a shower of Zyklon-B?
"Sweet home of folk romance,
Hushed Yuletide innocence."
My Weltschmalz, 'tis of thee:
Jackboot reality.
"No, no, more starry-eyed, more comradely.
Home of the Christmas tree,
Hearth that invented Santa and blonde tresses.
Don't leave out heart: heart's moonlit inwardnesses."
Watching the green go brown-
Shirt after Pan left town,
Hearing somnabulists on Gothic rooftops ringing
Dream bells, dream bells. —*"A Caligari Calvary?"*[2]
Cardboard dreams, stage bells,
Fairyland moaning in rut for a swanboat on
Wheels: it's then *he*
Shivered
Under a cookie-cutter moon of poisoned marzipan.

4. (son's outburst of prose quotes: *Footsteps of Doves*)
   His last letters of around January 1889 (signed 'Dionysus' and 'The

Crucified') urged 'doing away with Kaiser Wilhelm, Bismarck, and all anti-Semites' and urged Europe's rulers to form 'an anti-German league to sew up the Reich' lest its coming racist nationalism barbarize the world. Another 1889 letter damned his sister Elizabeth (in 1933, along with Cosima, a personal friend of the Führer) for spreading 'the damnable German anti-Semitism, this poisonous boil of national neurosis.' Already earlier, he urged a cosmopolitan 'good Europeanism' to save civilization from Richard Wagner's metapolitical romanticism, calling it a Nordic 'lance against civilization . . . a dictator in the name of the German Chosen People leading the Jews to slaughter as scapegoats of every possible public and private woe.' To his countrymen he added: 'Deutschland über alles, that was the end of German philosophy. Culture and the state are enemies . . . The Germans think that strength must reveal itself in hardness and cruelty; then they submit with ecstasy, are readily rid of their pitiful weakness, and devoutly enjoy Terror. That there is strength in mildness and stillness they do not readily believe. Yet the thoughts that guide the world come with the footsteps of doves.' By 1889, when the doctors locked him up, his forebodings had reached the climax: 'I was crucified by the German doctors . . . I am having all anti-Semites shot.'[3]

5. (you: 1914 & 1939)
"Crying 'stabbed in the back' or 'encircled and trapped,'
Having sowed what they feared, they tripped.
If that's how a couple of Reichs got scrapped,
What dream twice botched their script?"

(son's reply: 1945)
Two wars. They dreamed they played
Siegfried. The fire brigade
Found only bunkered Hagen,
Compulsively replayed.

(you: Coincidences)
"Nomen omen: swastika is Hakenkreuz;
You make it sound like Hagenkreuz.
Make something of this: was your warner around to warn
When the Schicklgruber-Hagen he warned against was born?"

(son's reply: *1889*)
Centennial of lib-eq-frat.[4] A Norn
Is crossing two dark threads, the old and torn
In bedlam. The new (is an age named *Nathan* burning?)
Slouches from Bayreuth towards Braunau to be born.

6. (you, then son: *The Kali Banality of Evil*[5])
"The torn one admitted he'd 'rather clown than be
Saintly.' " —Saints bleed too publicly.
"Admit he admitted (when his soothsaying raised so much hell)
He 'should have stuck to his verses.' "[6] —Though to sing
Till the end is sooth's beginning,
Yet at a midpoint exorcists must break
Even their lyre for the tribe's sake.
"Which cheers Caliban anyhow."
Prophet's throes, prophet's throne.
"Some throne! Eleven years of padded cell.
Half vegetable,
He slept into 1900, all the while
Preening—hoho—as king." —So, once, did I,
With letters I and N and R and I;
Who else so shared my second deriding crown
The day I became a lampshade?[7] . . . Brother clown,
The century you slept into, you woke.
Who else but you foresaw they'd puff my smoke
Up the same chimney their Santa Kitsch went down?

7. (Backdrop of barbed wire, shovel, ditch; son to young feminine you: *Song
   Till the End*)
If blossoms could blossom
One petal of petals
To whom all other blooms are
As leaves are to flowers,
It would be to the others
As you are, my daughter,
To all other daughters
Whom songs are adoring.
For what am I here for

If not to make love-songs
Of all the world's beauty
Whose birthday we share?

If rarest of fragrances
Brewed from aloofness
Too frail a quintessence
To ever be breathed,
It would be to the others
As you are, my daughter,
To all other daughters
Whom songs are encircling.
For what am I here for
If not to weave lassoes
Of song for the lonely
To tug them to love?

Say yes to the breezes.
If any dishevels
One curl of a ringlet,
I'll know and be with you.
The grace-notes that feather
The wing-beats of longing
Are lead till they heal with
Their singing your crying.
For what is a song for
If not to smooth ringlets
Of daughters too hurt by
The prose of the world?

When storms replace breezes,
No hurt can have healing.
Then the love I now sing you
Can pillow your fading.
For what am I here for
If not to link fingers
With daughters whose wistfulness
Worlds never answer?

For what is a song for
If not to stretch hands out
To signal the falling,
'You're never alone'?

When the Camp says: 'Dig graves now,
We're coming to shoot you,'
I'll help with your shovel
—(I'll know and be with you)—
To give you more seconds
To look up from digging
To look at the sun while
I pillow the sand out.
For what is love here for
If not to smooth ditches
For all the world's daughters
Whose dying we share?

PART THREE

---

*I obey my Dionysian nature, which does not know how to separate nega-
tion from affirmation.*

—Nietzsche, *Ecce Homo*

*Necessary to understand the god as inseparable
from the satyr . . .*

—Nietzsche, *Ecce Homo*

Prologue

I. (father)
Your father who takes no side
Faces the eighth day satisfied.
When gods are touchable and touch is godly,
Not till then are toys untied.

    1. (son)
    You, father, who look aside
    Assume blank faces on the toys you tried.
    I have learnt different, being sent inside.
    Too late to make man button-eyed.

II. (voice of feminine you, flung Godward through cloud curtain: *Like Boaz*)
"Numb God who made empathy girlish, are the star-cogs you spin with such fuss
Clockwork, not growth?

Till bounded by woman's dense circles, your Big Bang infinities fizz
Infinite froth.

Your ever lonesomer winters, pawing her pairings, undress
Green-smocked earth.

Your eons, they're ogling her hour—they ache for her April caress,
Recharging the warmth

Of all your drained cosmos: like Boaz, must cold-foot Entropy press
A hot-water bottle named Ruth?[1]

Evolution presents her new baby, nicknamed God's Image; come bless
Amoeba's aftermath;

'Stuff it down the toilet, it's human,' you chuckle benignly; 'the mess is
But amoeba's afterbirth.' . . .

Turning swine into men by casting them pearls, wives daily reverse
Your Circe myth.

Am I a sphinx or a sphincter? What does woman want?[2] *Less*
Of flame's hearth, of flame's moth.

Albino God, patron of fungus, you—with your envy of birth-force—
Forced birth pangs on birth.

Squeamish butcher, taste in your bloodbaths a bleeding of Eve you can't face:
Moon-wound's witch broth.[3]

Gag, barren sky, on my tribute: the wine of my monthly yes
To fertile earth-truth.

All night, all night, poor God, your pure and deathless breath—
Like sprayed underarm daintiness—

Stinks deader than death."

CYCLE FOURTEEN:
Mek

In the day ye eat thereof . . . ye shall be as gods.
—serpent in Genesis; 3:5

Hal wes thu, folde: firs modor.
Beo thu growende on godes faethme.
(Hale be thou, earth: men's mother.
Be thou fruitful in god arms.)
—oldest English earth prayer

Thus I: faltering forward,
Leaves around me falling,
Wind oozing thin through the thorn from norward
And the woman calling.
—Thomas Hardy, "The Voice"

The brutal-brittle k-sound "mek" (prehistoric Hittite word for "power") crunched into English—via Sanskrit and Greek—as "mechanical," and the MEK cycle assumes a connection between the machine power of metal and the disestablishment of woman. Imagine this cycle's you-voice as a male lab boss of aggressive technic achievement.

---

1. (you, then son: *Know-how*)
*"I've jetted loose from stone-age Cain, and haven't.
Was it a spark from his flint that sparked me to Mars?"*

147

The more ingenious the tool, the cruder the hand.
"Did the caveman who genius'd the wheel, stop painting the wall?"
Caliban wasn't Caliban, Prospero was.

I. (father, then you: *Vintage Season for the Old Adam*)
Eve spat a seed on mulch most fit,
On dungheap of her macho ape.
*"How odd—look up—that an apple pit
Has grown a mushroom shape."*

* * *

(Corny plaintive wailing music off-stage. Mother Goose waddles behind
yoū, crooning *The Global Lobotomy Blues;* capitalized syllables are louder
and linger over vowels:)
Little boy GEI-ger, come BLOWWW your horn;
The beep's in the meadow, the borsht's in the corn. [1]
Rockabye fall-out, on top of the show;
When the wind blows you, the tuna will glow. [2]
When the nerve BREAKS, Humpty Dumpty will fall.
Down will come BAAA-by, planet and all.

* * *

(you, then father: *Ecology*)
"I date earth Anno Domini."
You've left it ano homini.

2. (you, then son: *Machine Oil*)
"Once earth hick; hub of cosmos now."
Local chunkiness once. Chartres. Lascaux.
"I have been spontaneous in Bermuda."
Oil in your veins instead of.
"Speedways to." —Gloves between you and.
"My jackboots—" —Hide Achilles' heel.
*"Once I had me a dark night of the soul;
It must of been something I et."*
What, while it lasted, was it like to be man?

* * *

(you-reminiscence: *It Was Good to Have Been
Man*)

"After eight thousand years among the stars
Nostalgia—suddenly—for August
Tugged me like guilt through half a cosmos
Back to a planet sweet as canebrake,
Where winds have plumes and plumes have throats,
Where pictures
Like 'blue' and 'south' can break your heart with hints.

"After a mere eight flickers, nothing changed there
Among the birds, still just as blazing,
Among the lilt of leaves on rivers,
The heartbreak of the south and blue,
The canebrake-sweet of August night;
No change till
I, changeling, asked the natives: 'Oh my people,

" 'After eight cycles, how is this you greet me?
Where is my horse? Where is my harp?
Why are the drums of goat-skin silent?
Spin my abyss of resin-wine;
Drape me my coat of prophecy;
My name is——.'
Forgot it, I forgot it, the name 'man.' "

* * *

(son, then you: *She, He*)
Flashback to tribal dawn:
Cave nights, cave lights.
From that first campfire, two rival flame-lines:
Hers round, and yours——. —*"I hack roads straight."*
Steel fungus. . . . Her sleep wakes grass.
"Overwakes. When chortling in cahoots with wheels
I seal whole countrysides in eight-lane tar,
Grass curves its gross graffiti through."

Her circle warms the rain.
"My trio—Will-male-steel—
Glows livelier than her warmth."
Lively is not alive. A funeral pyre

Feels snugger than a hearth
A while.

II. (you, then father: *Yet Threshes*)
"Our bog of goggle-eyes begs for an era
Of drowse." —So minnows pray to beaks of gannets.
"More air, more air: our gasp from terra."
One of the uninhabitable planets.
When you who are, learn whose you are,
The austerest chin-lines sag,
Like keels of sunken flagships, once so precious.
"We're a cauldron of lips and tongues: to spawn or as snack?"
Meat either way rubs meat. —*"Yet threshes*
(Alone when most a pair)
For love that's more than hunger."
Your 'more' keeps murdering longer
For love than carnivore
For flesh. —*"Flesh, gulping flesh, is—"*
Sated. How sate a holy war?

3. (Son sets up placard, labeled: "TERRA'S MANIFESTO: 'Nothing human is alien to me.' " You—white-smocked as lab boss—set up rival placard: "MEK MANIFESTO: 'Engineers are the priests of a new epoch, without superstitions.' "[3] You, then son: *Terra Incognita*)
"Why uninhabitable planet?"
Why uninhabitable woman?
"Why can't geometry meter geo?"
Why not be blind enough to read earth's Braille?
"Nothing mek is alien to me."
Rack's priest now priest of tech.
"Old holy water, new formaldehyde
Her two preservers." —Her preservatives.
"Old church, new lab both map her
Dark continent: two telescopes—"
Up skirts of Terra. Two peeping (Saint) Thomases.
"Yet we, black robe or white, it's we who shield her,
Sealing her round and round in starched perfection

Of froufrou petticoats." —It's earth who,
When covered, quakes. One restless flounce
Shakes all your churches, labs, and other dirndls.
"Uncovering what?" —To find it, close your eyes
And follow the most archaic of your senses.
"No, no, my headcold—" —All engineers have colds.

III. (you to flying machine, then father)
"Brave new machine, 'tis I, thy Luddite lover,
Still splitting metal mind from gothic[4] heart,
Medievally mod. Solve contradictory me.
Or crash me; I can't get off." —Five hundred years now,
Heart is a jet-propelled sitdown strike.

    4. (son to you)
    Different once. Once—from passionate parch—
    Renewal, the shared instant: enter
    Queen Ge, King Helios.

      (Female and male stride in ceremoniously as son, father, and you
      leave. Sun king to earth queen: *Autumn Serenade*)
If through a wind I ripple every tide
With such a wave as rattles every quay,
It is to haunt the true lost flesh they hide;
All sea, all soil but sheathe my bride from me.

Her skirt of colored seasons crowns her thighs
And circles round the lunar tune she sways.
. . . O loose your tousled locks with drowsy grace
And slowly brush their green across my eyes.

Twisting your shoulder-blades beneath the plough
That fondles you when apple twigs are bent,
Deep in your hills you would not huddle so
If you believed how sad I am you went.

Then let no princeling of the apricots
Excite you with the ripeness of the year.
His nectared cheeks must burst; your courtier rots;
The snows are on his trail, will soon be here.

My scorch remains. And nibbles listlessly
A ghaut of all the wives of all my whims.
Autumnal tawny harems burn for me.
Such games will not distract me from your limbs.

Call to me dawdlingly when summer falters.
Attract me bitterly through molten grain.
I am the groom; look up, my clouds are altars
To worship you with desecrating rain.

   (earth to sun: *Counter-Serenade: She Invokes the Autumn Instant*)
Then touch the park; the leaves are stained to lùre you.
The leaves are spread on winds they fan befòre you.
They drained the summer, and their veins prefèr you,
Dark with the season they are keening for.

Then bring the heavy dying they prefer.
Each painful fruit is hanging heavier.
Why pause when loveliness grows lonelier
And love is just as melting as it looks?
There's but one touch that all the ripeness lacks:
You are the instant; you are waited for.

Then never wait when flutes of foliage bear you
Home on the homeward tune they always bore.
Fear not at all the twigs of flame they bear.
These never meant to be a barrier.
The lovely are as lonely as their gleam,
The lonely just as loving as they seem,
The fruits as melting as they always were:
There is a fondling they are furtive for.

Then touch my park. The leaves have spread befòre you
The green they drained, the darkness they prefer.
Come to the leaves, reach out and touch them all.
Bring to the smoldering year, that hovers fòr you,
The hovering instant love is dawdling for:

There's not one leaf that does not long to fall.

(Stainless-steel bulldozer clears stage of gods. You, then son: *Bulldozing:*)
  "What, then, is Mek to Ge?"
  What's hysterectomy?
  "Steel versus woman?"
  And snow against rain.
  "White-prone—hence black-prone—even in green,
  Can I tell queened snow from rain's warm queen?"

  (You alone, urgent-voiced: *Snow Against Rain*[5])
  "I bring a message from the rain.
  The addressee is green.
  My rain-queen sister has a twin
  Whose loam's not loam but steel.
  Steel cogs inside? A clockwork bride?
  Too soon to argue with the tide;
  Too late to warn the grain.
  My sister's sister's sun is snow.
  Let me go.
          *   *   *
  Who crushed a toad to pack a hill
  To throne—beyond the tick of wheels—
  A bride who but twinned a queen?
  Accuse, accuse. But whom? Rain whirls
  Bleak round that hill and mum.
  I didn't do it—ask below.
  I did, but let me go.
  Noon bleeds to dusk, too numb to heal;
  Snow is sun's bitterer name.
          *   *   *
  Resins are rivers untied,
  Flowing untowed uphill,
  Restoring noon.
  Snowfields—red sprinklings on white,
  The pounce on the lark on the run—
  Outdarken dark.
  Roots too frozen for tide,
  Twigs of a nest of a wren,

Vines reaching for rain
Sink under hail, under heel.

        *   *   *

Can rains, compelling tide,
Warm back estranged terrain?
Frail pact. One wrenching note
And trust lets go.
The toad I crushed to pack a hill
To footstool for a bride
A throne beyond the crush of snow
Has wrenched the voice of rain."

CYCLE FIFTEEN:
Core

Vegetable frenzies, I their core
—"you,"
triggering this intermezzo of new voices

The rhythm in a sparrow and a bud . . .
That pumped a spring into the veins of dance.
—Colin Reid, *Open Secret*

New voices: trees, stone, water. No father or son voices
in this cycle, and you only at start and epilogue.

(lungfish-you, briefly back again: *Vegetable Frenzies*)
"Who in his skin—speak, skeleton—
Is not a running tree? We've been
Bloomed by some primal restlessness on the run,
Inciting shape after shape after shape,
The gamut of stone, plant, ape.
As I sprout a lung's first draft above the wet,
I forget—no, I remember—my earlier zoom,
Launching the vegetable frenzies from algae to oak,
Choking the globe and I their core. A conch,
The throat I had not yet grown,
Was droning an unrest of seed,

155

A green before gill was or gut.
Throat, mourn
> *exultantly*
The peace lost when sea begot seaweed,
The hour birth got born."

                    *   *   *

INTERMEZZO of new (nonhuman) voices: tree and vegetables frenzies and then stone and river. The changes of indentation—unlike elsewhere—are not changes of speaker, there being no dialogues in the intermezzo, no father-son-you.

a. (willow sapling addressing humanity: *I Alone Am Moving*)
You all are static; I alone am moving.
Racing beyond each planted Pullman wheel,
            I pity you and long to reel
You through my thousand outstretched ways of loving.
Are you alive at all? Can non-trees feel?

Run while I may, for at my pith gnaws night.
The winds—these are great stacks of anchored air;
            I thresh them with my hard-pronged hair;
I jump right through them, roaring my delight.
Live while I may—run, run, no matter where.

How marvelous, if you but knew, is speed!
You all must wait; I am your overtaker.
            Striding to green from yellow acre,
I toss you spring. Each dawn, my tendrils knead
Stars into pancake-suns like a tall baker.

Trudging toward snowtime, I can mope for hours
To think of birds, the birds I leave behind.
            Why has the Spore Queen kept you blind
While granting sight and sentience to my flowers?
Black questions in my sap outwear my rind.

Bipeds (I almost envy you your peace)
Are free of this gnarled urge for absolutes

Which sweetens and saddens all my fruits,
Dragging my twigs down when I'd fly toward bliss—
While bugs and diamonds agonize my roots.

*   *   *

b. (same willow, older, at biped-felling ritual: *The Slacker Apologizes*)
We trees were chopping down the monsters in the
      Street to count their rings.
Who blessed our war? The oak invoked: 'Within Thee
Crush, Mother, quakingly these red-sapped things
        Whose burrowings
Foul Thy clean dung. Kill, kill all alien kings.'

Crowned by black moss or by obscener yellow,
      The flowerless monsters stood
On soil-blaspheming asphalt. How they'd bellow
Each time we lopped them—just as if their crude
        Numb root-pairs could
Feel feeling. O Goddess, the glory of being wood!

Then games of peace. Who was the poet? I.
      I was the willow lyre.
Even the oak was awe-struck; melody
Maddened whole meadows like a forest fire
        To hear my choir
Of leaves beat, beat, and beat upon each wire

Of winds I tamed and tuned so artfully
      It seemed an artless game.
You weed back there, don't think I didn't see
You yawning. Bored? Well, try to do the same.
        What? Suddenly lame?
Come, come, step and sing—or wither in shame.

Then crooned the crass young weed: 'Last night my stamen
      Could hear her pistil sigh.
Though far the orchard that her petals flame in,
We touched in dreams the hour that bee flew by.

My pollen's shy
Deep nuzzling tells her: weeds must love or die.'

Fools. How they cheered. But wait, I set them right:
    'Verse, verse, not poetry.
Jingles for jungles; grosser groves delight
In honey, but educated tastes decree
        Austerity.
True art is bitter, but true art sets free.

'True art, how can I serve you half enough?
    Had I a thousand sprays
And every spray a thousand sprigs, they'd sough
For beauty, beauty, beauty all their days—
        And still not praise
Not half the whirlwind-wonder of your ways.'

At this the oak, our captain, roared me down:
    'Mere beauty wilts the will.
Why are we here? To sing and play the clown?'
The forest answered: 'We are here to kill.
        With monsters still
Lurking, root out the murk upon our hill—

By feeding willow wood to . . . Beaverville.'
    My leaves drooped red: 'Right's wrong;
Bloom's ugly, being frail, and oaks look strong.
My inward seasons can't defy forever
        Thy outward weather:
Ax me down, Mother, for the guilt of song.'
        *   *   *

c. (pine—under spotlight in center stage—to rose: *My Gentlest Song*)
Remember, friend, your dancing-days of May
When restless willows rustled just for you?
You tossed your petals such a reckless way
You hardly noticed me the whole month through
And thought your beauty was its own defense.

Yet all the while my boughs were roof to you,
Bark raked by hail so you could sip the dew.
You know the zephyrs, I the hurricanes.
I've loved you fresher than my youngest cones
Because my crest needs nearer light than sun's.
Although I've died so many times each fall
That something of me cannot die at all,
Each ring of ripeness costs me dear
In chills you'll never feel who last a year.
Now go—goodbye—while I grow still more tall;
You wilt me when you look so glum,
For there's one shade I must not shade you from.

Small friend, you'll never leave me when you leave,
Though yours the seared and mine the phoenixed leaf.
My reverent hunger waits for you, it waits
To weld us even closer than before
We sprouted (toward such different fates),
Close as the hour we lay there, spore by spore,
Two seeming clones in selfsame garden bed.
How many times I've wished me dead instead;
How gladly I'd divide my unspent sheen
And lend your ebb my evergreen.
But must not spare you, even if I could,
For it's not I who made you less than wood.
You—bright brief putrefying weed—
Will feed my roots next spring, will feed
The fabulous white-hot darkness of my core.

                    *   *   *

d. (After pine is prematurely felled by lightning, gnarled old cactus sets up
    desert backdrop, scorns spotlight, and addresses modern you: *Paysage
    Moralisé*)
    I'm the earned ouch of the heel of strut.
My health is parch, my moral code is slash.
    Root-anchored only when you watch me,
I caper and mimic behind you when you don't.
    The desert—crammed into my crouch—

Austerely fells luxuriant posturers,
    Their love more callous than my hate.
I'm all the targets where your barbs land facing
    Outward, a reverse Sebastian,
A retribution of boomerang porcupines.
    My core's unfabulous prose-truth warns you
How justly man is aimed at by his aims,
    How in the archeries of ego
A target is a mirror is a scales.

                    *   *   *

e. (a small potato, overlooked by all: *The Insulted and the Injured*[1])
I, underground giant, waiting to be fried,
Of all your starers the most many-eyed:
What furtive purpose hatched me long ago
In Indiana or in Idaho?

In Indiana and in Idaho
Earth-apples—deadlier than Eden's—grow,
Puffed up with buried will-to-power unguessed
By all the duped and starch-fed Middle West.

In each Kiwanis Club on every plate,
So bland and health-exuding do I wait
That Indiana never, never knows
How much I envy stars and hate the rose.

You call me dull? A food and not a flower?
Wait! I'll outshine all roses in my hour.
Not wholesomeness but hubris bloats me so
In Indiana and in Idaho.

Something will split (as all potatoes know)
When—once too often mashed in Idaho—
From my drab husk the shiningest of powers
Rises—
            (I'm sun, I fill the sky)—
            and lours.

f. (an idyllic gallows pastorale, spoken to its fruit by the oak of "Salt" in
   cycle seven: *To My Playmate, with Thanks for All Those Carefree Days Together*)
You are my winter comfort, loyal fruit
That never tumbles from this hempen twig.
My flowers, for all their sun-time vows, elope
With the first snowflake; green frays off so quick;
But (faithful to the sacrament of rope
That married blood and wood) you still remain
To dance me Mayward and unfrost my hope.
When too much longing droops me with the pain
Of too much beauty; when O once again
Caress of bugs—or diamonds?—stabs my root;
When doubt, and doubt of doubt, make sap congeal:
Then I'll just twitch my branch and you'll dispel
All spells by rattling me some joyous jig.

How glad-with-life you hop and swing and dangle.
Better to ride on wind than trudge on rock.
A nuzzling breeze rubs, purring, past your ankle;
Kind humble crawlers—once they feared your plow—
Now hiss affectionately from your throat;
Between your ribs a heart—a wren's—is hot.
All tears you ever lost, rain cries them back
Into your sockets. Gongs of starlight spangle
Your tar^2 with tintinnabulating dew—
Till black and gold and music fuse for you,
In liquid loud mosaics round your brow.

What prose and platitude and meanness clogged
Your head before the black ones pecked it pure!
Next, worms and weather scrubbed the nerve-webbed mesh
Of ego out. This was a filthy chore.
Now you're a hive for honeybees. They flocked
To sweeten and to resurrect your skull.
Today it hums with dreams more beautiful
Than tuneless lusts that stung your brain before.
How long, O fruit, since ripeness burst your skin?
Commemorate that second birth. You bore

What every triviality of flesh
Is pregnant with: the perfect bone within.

            *   *   *

g. (Locale: the "Vinland" continent discovered by Leif Erikson, 1,000 A.D.
   Same oak, now a pirate plank, chants these Old Norse runes to the count-
   less captives who must tread on him: *Saga*)
      You must walk the plank.
I can guess why you're not in a hurry.
      (You must walk the plank.)
While you walk, I'll creak you my story
    —*(You must walk the plank)*—
Of my rise from old wood to new glory.
      (You must walk the plank.)
You will hear only me till the hop.
      (You must walk the plank.)
Take pride in my rise as you drop.

     Vinland the Good!
Guzzling her fjords, I woke.
     Vikings gulped
Her mead in skulls and spoke:
     'Of all the fjeld
Be thou our gallows oak.'
     Years flew by,
More swift than the crows on my fruit
     Till Wyrd decreed
A doom of ax at my root.

     Thankless thanes:
I had served with such loyal joy.
     Was felled because
Had frightened the milksop boy
     Of a doting jarl.
The dotings began to cloy
     When the gloating babe—
Did I ask him to watch so near?—
     Was crushed by my crash.
I was sawed to serve as his bier.

Years crawled by,
More slow than the worms in my fruit,
   Till coffin-ghouls
Smashed me to look for loot.
   Then chapmen came:
'This lid will stanch our boat.'
   Not quite. The leak
I wrought proclaimed I frowned
   On burgher mart.
The only carl not drowned—

   —was a thief in the brig
Who clung to me when they sank.
   I wrought him dreams
Till he rose to pirate-chief's rank.
   He knighted me
The skald of plop: Sir Plank.
   I wrought revolt:
He walked me, too. How sweet
   Is fear's last squeal,
The sweat I taste through feet.

   Gallows and crash,
Coffin and treacherous leak.
   Not bad in their way.
But these diving-board days are my peak.
   (*You must walk the plank.*)
Every man's tread is unique:
   Some grudging, some gay;
Some bouncing, some needing a shove.
(*Here's goodbye; here's the edge of the edge of the plank.*)
I'll remember each footstep with love.

h. (stone: *I Am an Old Town-Square*)
Come near—rebuild me, hear me.

                   History wrapped her
Calamities round me in a sevenfold quilt,
Whose layers are towns. A crass and tinny scepter,
Such as the brasher kind of dynasts tilt,

Is all my courtyard holds of my first tribe.
Their names? Their fame? No interesting guilt
Of overreach coaxed footnotes from a scribe;
Their centuries were rain my gutter swilled.

Such songless trudgers it was joy to jilt.
I became a dirge black crows, black coffins shrilled.
Plague was my second town. Plague snowed those black
Song-notes across my granite music rack.

Next, pilgrims found that coffinwood and built
A pleasure town of feasts and lusts. (My third.)
Five hundred years they belched and strewed their milt.
What did time save of them? One dried up turd.

A trade-town's fourth, with art so polychrome—
Such loftiness from huckstering distilled—
That sudden shaggy nomads, wolfskin-frilled,
Would rather starve there than be khans at home.

My fifth town downright pranced with buccaneerings.
Loot gave my cobblestones a jingly lilt.
The night my floor was starry-skied with earrings,
Sackfuls of earlobes clogged my drains like silt.

My sixth was reared by knights who hanged those raiders.
Its saintly prayer was, 'Vengeance to the hilt.'
Gouged by Love's camp of gallows and crusaders,
My scars were chinks where armored knees have knelt.

Time passed. Those chinks lodged clover. Smoke said, 'Wilt.'
Desert of smokestacks. But a bee had smelt
A bud, and soon my seventh town consoled
My claws of soot with rings of buzzing gold.

A dream:—*From eighth cocoon my airiest city*
Spreads glittering wings, true gold now, nothing gilt.
Around me twirls a tinkling live confetti
Of childhoods. Ancient pavements bask fulfilled;

And rustling down each twilight, slim on porches,
Tiptoe on spires like willowy stilt on stilt,
Shimmers of girlhood—aspen glances—pelt
My yard with fireflies from soft-browed torches.

A dream . . . it never came. Bombs came. Bombs spilt.
Sweet Geiger sirens[3] sing for you, my hearer.
But where's my lost eighth town? Get me rebuilt.
My stones await you radiantly. Come nearer.

*   *   *

i. (river: *The First Morning*)
Around the curve where all of me that fountained
Leans over on its side and is a stream
And loiters back the long, the round-about,
The sweet, the earth way back to sea again—
At just that curve I woke.

What is awakeness?

A thing I own? Or opened eyes that own me,
Sobbing me through as if my banks were lids?
I only know I'm freed to be less free:
A tear of longing on a cheek of loam.

Before that flash, I sleepwalked through my circle
(Sea, river, cloud, then rainfall back to sea)
While never feeling how it feels to feel.
I have no memory of what came before
Except a silver sandy sense of glide—
And this odd shame: one eon mill wheels chained me.
The chainers didn't last; I did, I do.

Who took flow's casualness? I never thirsted
To symbolize or mean. Who took my sleep?
Leaves fall on me as light as sunbeams; even
Boulders are weightless; only meanings weigh.
I am a river and a river only.
But now, since waking, not of water only:
A tic of knowing on being's blank blind brow.

Faster. I skid between the rocks like breezes
Between the leaves. I skim the rocks so lightly
I now seem less a river than a breath.
Or is this hurtling airiness a warning
(How can I know yet, being so young awake?)
That I have reached my final waterfall?
Too late to stop; enslaved by back and forth;
No rest for me in either blue. My tiptoes
Of dew creep up and stub against the clouds;
And clatter down again; again to clamber.
Green-drifting pools and lulls below, goodbye;
Intimate riverbed, joy of the touch of a contour,
Clinging to me you never will climb with me now.
Stay with me seaward: earth-half of my circle.
But cloudward (stript of shores, a ghost of vapors)
Each strives alone. And now I flex my sinews
For stream's last jump—I clear the rocks—I fall
To rise.
            No, not yet fall; not rise; suspended
One hovering instant, I'm the world's first morning
(Everything possible, not yet in groove)
And stream's first jump.
                        The hover ends. I move.

Epilogue To Core Cycle

Yet the thoughts that guide the world come with the footsteps of doves.
　　　　　—Nietzsche, *Thus Spake Zarathustra*

Only so much of the Dionysiac-Bacchic substratum of the universe may enter an individual consciousness as can be dealt with by Apollonian transfiguration; so that these two prime agencies must develop in strict proportion. Whenever the Dionysiac forces become too turbulent . . . Apollo is close at hand. . . . Let us sacrifice in the temple of both gods.
　　　　　—Nietzsche, *The Birth of Tragedy From the Spirit of Music*

(End of nonhuman intermezzo. Enter feminine you, echoing the
　preceding river voice: I—*Mediatrix*)
"Apollo's large orb; red orblets of Bacchus;
And I the connecting, the reconciling
River,—the light-god's light fulfilling
All unripe grape-globes.
But
　why must a woman, though even high priestess,
Be ever through others fulfilling her tides?
Feathers of nestings, hexes of fathers,
Fetters of hormones, Eva's whole backpack,
All's let me down.
Silk handcuffs today; but tomorrow
How will it be when I step in the clearing,
Not doe into headlights but lightning from cloud?
Will I joke with typhoons the way scavenger-crones

Chat with breezes? Will heroes I'm shrining
Shrine my lap, shrine my brow? Will the bridges I burn
Be my stilts? Ah till then, till tomorrow,
I—mediatrix, renewer—"

(renewed male you, facing river: *Release*)
"Was ever blue such fever-quelling blue?
Slope of her cheekbones, now a landscape's cheek,
What else but she, translated into river?
One summer I had a sister used to tilt
Her head a little in a haze of ease;
She's now that sky-reflecting glide down there,—
Strewn acorns the planets nesting on her blue.

Just be (she hinted), be; outlast, not grasp;
All race toward slag and waste; be lag, not haste.
. . . Then I saw thistle-fluff nestling in storms that batter and
Plant it. Her peace (too casual for redeemers)—
Like dewfall, uninsistent—rippled twice:
A shimmer of shoulder first, then shrug of fountain,
To her own self enough; yet more, yet more.

Was ever drift such din-dissolving drift?
Vine god with form god: rival temples once,
Linked wellsprings now, her undulance their hyphen,
Form flowing as wine, wine formed as vein of marble:
Core once again core, laws once again laws. Released from
Unmerry-go-round of shape after shape after shape,
I—feather—tread carpets of storm on a dance floor of graves.

My sister moved where words stopped short, recording
But this: there stones in any ditch are wings,
There clods comb back like clouds, there will lets go.
Am I the stone, the slinger, or the sling?
I tried to twirl her round my storms of will;
She tried to curl me round her trance of lull;
Then dawn and traffic bustled loud between;—

—but now no longer. Passage through. To where?
Last night, rain whispered 'soon' (was it hope, was it panic?);
'Tomorrow,' whimpered the storms and exulted the waters;
This morning I'm shaking with awe that has no object,
Feeling a path, a far one, very near.
To what? No blaze—I beg—no blaze for one
Soul-sick too often of too garish noon.

No blaze, no dawn descends but frenzy's end."

CYCLE SIXTEEN:

Choose

Sweet and sweet is their poisoned note . . .
Ever singing, 'die, oh! die.'
Young soul, put off your flesh, and come
With me into the quiet tomb;
Our bed is lovely, dark, and sweet.
                    —Thomas Lovell Beddoes, *The Ivory Gate*

Il faut, voyez-vous, nous pardonner les choses.
. . . Et si notre vie a des instants moroses,
Du moins nous serons, n'est-ce pas? deux pleureuses.
                    —Paul Verlaine, *Romances Sans Paroles*

Charon: in Greek mythology, the grisly skipper who
ferries the dead across the river Styx into Pluto's underworld:
for the fee of an obol.
                    —*Dictionary of Classical Antiquities*

Speakers: in this dialogue of one, "you" split into two wrangling wraiths, "Self" and "Beddoes." This is a fictionalized Beddoes. The real one, nick-named "death's jester" and author of *Death's Jest-Book*, wrote none of these lines (save the above "poisoned note" and the lobster line) but might if . . .

A.

SELF: Birthday party . . . sixtieth . . . over. Alone at last.
    (Enter—from Self's forehead—Beddoes, arriving late—and in ferry-skipper costume—for the masquerade party.)

BEDDOES: Never alone.

SELF: Are you ghost or guest?

BEDDOES: Your (every scribbler's) other. Here to
  Make you choose between . . . you know which two.

SELF: That publicized pair? I won't deign to say
  Scribbler's most purple double-cliché.

BEDDOES: Don't say it; just nickname them D. and L.
  Flesh being purple, they won't go away.
  Your L. is a dreary wedding knell
  While my D.—ah, there's a blithe funeral bell.

SELF: Watch your adjectives, Beddoes; they're bias prone.
  P.R. man for graveyards, your hangups are known.

BEDDOES: L. or D., choose one.

SELF: But which, Beddoes, which, Beddoes, which of the pair?

BEDDOES: Which . . . is . . . stronger?
  (Clock starts striking twelve but at intervals so slow they last till
  dialogue's end.)

SELF: Which twelve: noon's lion mane, night's panther cape?

BEDDOES: Night's rot-sweet ripeness bears the stronger flower;
  What you call hemlock, we call headier grape.
  All unspoilt fruits taste sour.

SELF: I hear a ferry-skipper's throat—

BEDDOES: —sweet and sweet is my poisoned note—

SELF:—still singing, 'die, oh! die.'

BEDDOES: Did you hear that a box can be a boat?
  No more sky—

B.

SELF: —except blue coffin lid of lapis lazuli.

BEDDOES: Blue for whom? Lid's sides are two.
  We under, we miss the showier view.

SELF: Then why do skulls stare so?

BEDDOES: Eyes that face in
  Outsee you.

SELF: Frail weapon.

BEDDOES: Enough to woo
  You under. I win. No more green—

C.

SELF: —except skull's malachite and emerald sheen.
    Not just you
    Make bad taste a *Jest-Book;* watch me do it too:
    Here's an ivory wreath from a gourmet's teeth
    And bookworms gnawing God's vellum-bound Word
    And a gross grub hatched from an aesthete's turd.
BEDDOES: What's a lobster's tune when he's boiled?
SELF: Here's a big-headed embryo smirks debonair.
    Whose pubic fuzz is his boutonnière?
    Whose tummy his crematorium urn?
BEDDOES: It's his mommy!—see how their ashes burn
    Who in life were so icy a goodygood pair.
SELF: Here's a harp of ribs that a mole snout ripples—
BEDDOES: And a miser's metal a red rust nibbles—
SELF: And poppies, poppies,
                    tousled petal nipples,
    Bleeding black milk. And you: our catharsis
    Of terrors and pities, Pluto's grammarian.
BEDDOES: And you: when your word-crammed brow is carrion,
    You are the text the grave-worm parses.

D.

SELF: Not just you
    Sing beautiful dyings; I too, I too.
    These anthills of alphabet tingling my tomb,
    Are they editing time or rewriting my tome?
    These wingbeats of ravens tinkling my grief,
    Are they black snowflakes to tickle my grave?
    Are fungi the fingers the lepers slough off
    To stroke lovers buried alive?
BEDDOES: Soon stroke of twelve; quit stalling; choose.
SELF: Fetch, fetch me my pyre. I'll soon be so glad to woo D.
    That I'll chortle. Except when I retch.
BEDDOES: L. or D., D. or L.,
    Sockets are winking: from pelvis, from skull.
    Let snakes in—smash thighbones or brows.
SELF: I beg heart's faltering Morse,

'Can you hold out till twelve o'clock?'
It banters tauntingly, 'Of course
Not.'
BEDDOES: Dickory dock.
SELF: But . . . what's that laugh—from the past—outside?
BEDDOES: Forget . . . her. Try a . . . boat ride.
No more shore—

E.
SELF: —till bribed by coins—or souls?—you ferry for.
BEDDOES: Both trash. In turn I cure
Fever. I lower temperature.
SELF: Doc Charon, monk of the macabre,
Your greenless garden tempts me toward your harbor.
But . . . if a fever twining with a fever—
BEDDOES: Forget her and inhale my airless arbor,
Black bloom of coal, white bloom of fragrant mould.
Old man, your friends went ahead to the dark river.
Don't wait forever; quick, gulp its cure-all liquor;
Crush all your past—like fern in coal's dense wreath—
In one intense last breath.
SELF: Past? But . . . there's pain no Lethe's ether
Can censor. I want to . . . not forget her.
BEDDOES: Stop—let her fade or I fall—old fool, die quicker.
SELF: What earth-umbilic tether jerks me back
One global ripple before tick's last tock?
Suddenly (damn you, here's your obol)
I feel what I a thousand times did scribble
Unfelt: love is stronger than death.

(Beddoes wraith, exorcized, flees. One heartbeat later, Self's clock strikes
fatal twelve.)

CYCLE SEVENTEEN:
Toward

Why dois your brand sae drap wi bluid . . . ?
Sic conseils ye gave to me O.
—Scots ballad

A fool with thorn as crown made a crown of all thorn.
—"you" in this cycle.

Those who can't bear the sentence, "There is no salvation,"
ought to perish.
—from Nietzsche's posthumous notebooks

Speakers: father, his stagehand, and (in italics) male and female you-voices. No son voice; now and then son presence may be felt meddling.

I. (Enter father as spry old codger, sliding down from ceiling on fireman's pole and sniffing air.)
Armageddon weather. Dust versus duster.
   (you entering up from trapdoor)
"Name unseen third."
Respect my word-block against meddler.
"Dust's government-in-exile. Unseen, meddler gives
My dust a helping hand."
And your own hands? Heavy with what?
"I, too, have a right to a block."

Kid Cain, stone-sharpener, manicures his claws
Ever since.
"If I scraped a stone sharp,
It was only to build."
Still heavy with.
"Well, if I've shed—say, wood—
Listen, all gets shed; fur for example."
Ever heavier.
"What's gravity to me whose hands build wings?"
That stone.
"So long ago."
Long fuse.

II. (you-outburst, then father)
"Pure is
And treacherous my kaleidoscope of white on
Whitewash. Don't
Blurt unbleached pasts.
Go on strike, amoebas; manward is not to but
Toward, and every toward is too much from.
Yet golden pasts, continuities,
Wind-paw on wheat, sun-slant on rivers;
Not every flamingo is plastic.
She helped me up when.
Hands need to clasp, or.
O but heavy both my . . . with—
                    . . . ever heavier."
Some white stones don't stay white.

III. (father, then you)
You're the only toy I've somewhat . . . freed.—*"How free?"*
So free you'll scream for a chain when you see
(Through radar's round rays, at the end of curved space)
What goes on in the back of your head.
"In a bog eons back, too buried to heed,
Where horrors still hide, they discreetly face
Otherward."
That bog, it may churn you a face you can't chain.

"An invader? I'd better head homeward."
Try it. When safely home you've hied,
Where sur-real won't always stay sub,
You'll meet—with hate that's half a sob—
An other you'd rather not greet.
"I'll let in no other. Stained stars of which nobody heard
May have freaks who can face (at the end of curved space)
Some Jack-in-the-box in the back of their head.
But I curse what lurks under so monstrous a hide;
No good citizen needs such a hood."
All monsters—that's why you're all boring—have got
To play games. Why pretend you don't know?—*"Don't know what?"*
That he's not from the stars but the gory-hued
Same self you've always had.
"What's it called?"
Human.
"I'll . . . still stay sane."
Yes, you've that choice: stay dead. Or look-and-go-mad.
Jack-Ripper-in-the-box rips everything but
Inward.

＊　＊　＊

IV. (father to stagehand crew)
Natural selectors, police your beat;
Dismantle dinosaurs: ice age, retreat.
Debasement lab, match a crook-her-little-finger baboon in heat
With a grand-gesture yahoo who'll compose
A Ninth Symphony and Auschwitz while picking his nose.
Later their bed, when it stops creaking, is good—
Nature wastes nothing—for their coffinwood.

    (Male-you is joined by female-you, both now in baboon costumes.
    Crew disperses to its chores, except for archangel stagehand,
    who warns father:)
Meanwhile Adam and Eve, they found out about dying.
They're hopping around, hugging and crying.
She's bellyaching about some kind of undersize rain.

(she-ape singing)
"Westron wynde when wyll thow blow
The smalle rayne down can rayne
Chryst yf my love wer in my arms
And I yn my bed agayne."

(stagehand)
And now she blabs, *'Mother, I cannot mind my wheel'*[1];
And now, *'The lost traveller's dream under the hill.*[2]*'*
Meanwhile—what's this?—she plucks
Some kind of cigar box.

(she-ape with ancient lute)
"Brightness falls from the air;
Queens have died young and fair."[3]

(father)
That rubbish, she's making it resonant,
Slobbering to her slob,
As if one little case of finding out about dying
Were a doomed planet's victory sob.

(she turning toward stagehand)
"Dust hath closed Helen's eye.
I am sick, I must die."

(stagehand to father)
Do something, master; low morale in the ranks;
Stashing of haloes in Swiss banks.
She's contagious even to archangels; lyric means panic;
Compared to the she-threat, a Lucifer's merely Byronic.

(father unruffled)
Now I'm switching off her heart
To make a lab test of how apes part.

(She collapses. "You," still in baboon costume, clutches dead she-ape
and sings to her)

"How dark the veins of your temples;
Heavy, heavy your hands.
Deaf to my voice already
In sealed-off lands?
Under the light that flickers
You are so mournful and old,
And your lips are talons
Clenched in a cruel mold.
Silence is coming tomorrow
And possibly underway
The last rustle of garlands,
The first air of decay.
Later the nights will follow
Emptier, year by year:
Here where your head lay with gently
Ever your breathing near."

(father)
Such boohoo for just some blue-assed baboon
That I've switched off.

(stagehand:)
                                  Not so off. Her tune—?

(Their fur partly peels off; her voice from below her body:
Which of Us Two?)
"When both are armed with tenderness, too wild
With oneness to be severance-reconciled;
When even the touch of fingertips can shock
Both to such seesaw mutuality
Of hot-pressed opposites as smelts a tree
Tighter to its dryad than to its own tight bark;
When neither jokes or mopes or hates alone
Or wakes untangled from the other; when
More-open-than-skin, more-deep-than-gut are one
In marriage of the very skeleton;—

"When, then, soil peels mere flesh off half this love
And locks it from the unstripped half above,

How can I tell which side of soil I'm on?
Have I lain seconds here, or years like this?
I'm sure of nothing else but loneliness
And darkness. Here's such black as stuffs a tomb,
Or merely midnight in an unshared room,
Holding my breath for fear my breath is gone,
Unmoving and afraid to try to move,
Knowing only you have somehow left my side,

"I lie here, wondering which of us has died."

(father)
Trick of acoustics; ventriloquist palaver.
Meddler always messing with some cadaver.

(More fur peels. He-ape: *Rhythms of Obsession*)
"Kind as dew, calm of unfalling petals,
Motionless and recurring creek,
Mild park ambushing the ambler,
Warning the lover: 'Trespassing Required.'

The birds are so light when they land,
Land and hop a little,
So light on the blade of the pond-grass
That it sinks not at all, wings never touch water.

And the blade, the untroubled,
Never even trembling. The pond untingling. The park
Rippled only by the lover, by the rambler saying:

'Always the same.' How many times, sometimes with joy,
Has he not said it, and sometimes—'Always the same'—
Desperately? 'Always only that face.' "

(Last fur fading. Stagehand to father:)
You stopped her heart; how come her face won't stay
Terminal? How come they're peeling away?
How come, Mr. Big, when toys sing
Darkest, they're shining?

(father voice a bit anxious)
When song lights up her eyes like that and when
Her eyes light up their bodies, then—

(stagehand voice a bit less respectful)
Who's Mr. Creator around here, you or they?

V. (father, setting up movie camera labeled 'X-rated')
We'll see who's creating. I've drugged him a trance
Where blue flicks seem blue flowers of romance.[4]
    (Aiming camera at pair, father croons mock-romantically in olde-poesie
    style)
In dreams, you've wooed in the Sacred Wood,
But in fact you'll wed in coffinwood;
In dreams, lo in bowers of lovers true,
But in fact, in fact in movies blue—
    (giving you brusque shove)
Now spew.

    (you, voice enraptured, then father)
"Dice cup of wedlock, roll my genes and spout
Radiant generations out.
My facts are dream, my dreams are fact;
Love's fool gets saved in the last act."
If he lasts.—*"I've lasted through ape,*
Upstairs out of fish and mud,
Each thorn-crown a change of shape;
Now I mount to a snow-pure crown."
Ritual lamb, ritual knife, ritual clown
Of the guilt-dark temple of flood,
Re-enact me two rites of flow.
"Only one is the color of snow.
The other's the color of bl—.
Of blessings. All's white to hearts without stain."
Was white the color on your stone?

    (Stagehand fetches black coffin and paints it white. Father to stagehand)
Sharpen his knife and hers; say it's for wedding-feast carp.
Buffs call my slaughter-movies 'snuffs.'

(you with ecstatic ballet leaps, then father)
"My marriage to soul! Tonight reborn."
I'll drop the mask, you drop the corn;
It's not stairs but Mount Venus you'll 'mount.'
Come jet your fount; my movie runs
A Sermon not on the Mount but on the mons.[5]
"Sic conseils ye gave to me O."

(father voice rising to thunder)
Shut up and strip; reborn means porn;
Gods don't skip meat for Lent.

(you voice ever loftier)
"Do I hear Elfland's delicate horn?
With love that's half a sob,
My sacred rivers—eye, pore, pelvis—throb,
A Ganges every vent."

(father to stagehand)
So much for creators; I've baited the trap.

(stagehand)
On whom will it snap?

VI. (you voice of shy and anguished poise, what sometimes gets called 'dig-
     nity of man')
"Now all's in place . . . joy . . . JOY."
Toy . . . TOY. Fool, sing till you drop,
"Gods rise though they drop; we because we drop.
Because man kept dropping from lugging too much uphill,
A fool with thorn as crown made a crown of all thorn.
If she and I face and, yes, crown the porn that's our lot
Even though—just because—it debases pride's prop—"
Stop. Don't say it. Censors, cut.

(stagehand)
Sky holding its breath: is man a thing or . . . well, what?

(father)
It's his own choice cuts that knot.

(same shyly poised "you" voice)
"Clay was never indifferent, was always morality play,
Each tiniest choice of infinite voice.
At the limit, each time at our limit of utmost
Debasement, a rescuing rhythm—not rooftop but
Basement—almost breaks through, almost
Not. And the hover, the ever
Unresolved breakthrough, is rescue enough.
Soaring for more might . . . snuff me with air too rare.
I shall fear no evil so long as . . . her breathing is near."
     (kicking coffin from stage)
"Maybe God's the real Ripper; maybe it's he who's not facing
The clay he scarred.
Now the vomit returns to the dog, the scar to the dart;—
     (facing father)
"Now, artist of the razor, face your art."

     (father)
Catastrophe. Dense dot outweighing my
Hollow immensity. And he whom I once trusted most,
My first-born s—ss—
                       sunk self, arming them inmost.
And so I can't tempt them with lowdown pelf
Or oldfashioned Faust-bait of power and lust
To betray the twined roots of their life.
     (facing you)
But yours still the choice of—ah, loftily—tempting yourself
With soul booze. Crew, sharpen that knife.
     (thundering again)
ACHTUNG. Shed clothing. Blue movie, start whirling.

     (Crew sets up porn studio, noisy and crowded. You to her)
"All's quiet; we're completely alone, my darling."
     (you as father shines camera light above)
"Above us, our guardian stars twinkle like bulbs."
     (you voice coarsening, no longer shy)
"Already my nostrils sniff a whiff
From whiter planets. But not enough.
More, more! My meek lungs deserve gulps."

(father bringing back white coffin)

When the meek strut, a sniff earns a snuff.[6]

    (Father proffers shiny snuff-knife. Too inspired to notice, you absent-
    mindedly grab it:)

"I now choose the shining world-cuddle of all-loving-all,

Not the small private oneness of twos."

    (you with one foot on floor, one on unnoticed coffin)

"One foot still touches the globe I've spurned,

And one probes sky I've earned.

My titan stride enters soul, not bride;

I shed not clothing but her.

I'll need no human ties as I soar

Godward, Godward."

Cloudward.

"Man's climb from worm, my climb so warm,

Is it nestward, nestward?"

Westward.

"Where to, this maze from east to haze?"

Bedward.

"White sheets are wings; a saved fool sings.

But why am I shaking? It's not that cold.

Why palsied in horror? I'm not that old.

What's making me blurt what I've never quite said:

Why are my hands so . . . red, so red?"

Edward, Edward![7]

CYCLE EIGHTEEN:
Threads

_____

*King of the New Jerusalem in 1533 in Munster . . . was Jan Bockelsen
(John of Leyden). . . . Having announced that the Last Judgment was
at hand and that Munster alone would be saved, he declared himself
king of the whole world . . . calling on the poor to rise against the world
conspiracy of Antichrist, seen in the luxury and avarice of clergy and
nobility or Jews. . . . A direct line can be traced from the medieval
prophets of the millennium to both the Nazi and Leninist movements.
. . . Jan Bockelsen imposed a reign of terror proclaiming a rule of love.*
—The Observer, 1970

*"Two reasons Masons won't let me join: I'm Catholic and—"
You said two?
"And an atheist."
Aŋd or But?
"There is no God, and Mary is his mother."*
—George Santayana in conversation
with this writer, Rome, 1945

(Trialogue before undrawn curtain)
(you)

> *"Too long I've been the buffer-brother
> Through whom two prima donnas who don't address each other
> Address each other."*

(father)

> Moment's truce of beasts at waterhole to gather
> The threads, the threads.

184

(son)

    Our old motifs weave back to close the circle;
    Three straight lines bend.

(father)

    Not circle; new spiral, world without end.

(Father yanks up curtain; separate dialogues resume.)

         *   *   *

    1. (you, then son: *Threads Rethreaded*)
    "Your father who looks aside
    Assumed blank faces on the toys he tried.
    You have learnt different, being sent inside.
    In autumn only man is heavy-eyed."

    Toys don't know they're toys.
    If they do, they're not.
    A thing or not a thing?
    A circle or a dot?

    "Birth gape and death gape are inkpots.
    One two three, one two three, boom.
    Our life's but a Rorschach of ink blots
    Between an oom and an oom."

    Yet once between exit and enter,
    Between steps three and one,
    You, the waltz's center,
    Brush against sun.

I. (you, then father: more *Threads*)
"End of my upward-facing era:
Why waste more prayer on beaks of gannets?"
'More air' is still the lungfish-gasp of terra,
One of the uninhabitable planets—

"Where meat drinks meat, now milt, now milk, yet threshes
Alone when most a pair."

At least you'll see your Pilot face to face.
"But upside-down?"—Well, meathooks can't go bare.

"Is a man a bleeding throat of brine
Between a bed and a bed?"
The white that the rams go spilling,
Their steaks pay back in red.

"But in our dry aquarium of landfish
Some things are something else."
You'd drown in deserts on the brine you are.
"Till a clown dingdongs our pulse."

When you who are, learn whose you are,
You'll sag in underwater wobble.
How can a lonely spongy dot
Sop up all ocean?—*"Gobble, gobble."*

(father, facing appletree, then you)
That tree in the park I fenced,
Are you marching against its fruit?
"Not against its knowledge fruit; against
Its drier fruit: nailed wood."

 (Offstage voice of John the Baptist, Luke 3:9, crying in the wilderness:)
'Every tree therefore which bringeth not forth good fruit
Is hewn down, and cast into the fire.
And the people asked him, saying,
WHAT SHALL WE DO THEN?'

> 2. (shift of last threads to lone son, addressing you from Gethsem-
> ane: *The Applewood Ballad*)
> A garden got lost in a garden.
> Eden. Gethsemane.
> One seedling for apples or crosses.
> A tree found its way to a tree.
>
> Applewood climbing came easy.
> A gardener outdangled his fruit.

Left side, right side, honest gypsters.
The middle tree stole root.

If I forget thee, O womb stain, let my nose lose its cunning.
Glass flowers—let them try to beget.
After the hanging gardens,
My People forgot to forget.

Eons of stinkless Immaculate love
Parked at a cattle car.
One yellow for badge[1] or for manger.
A star found its way to a star.

Some bring me blood now, some champagne.
It was not what I asked on the hill.
O what poured into the shower room?
I wait for water still.

Applewood knowledge came flavored.
Vinegar. Zyklon-B.
One pilgrim staff hasn't reblossomed.[2]
It paces a garden with me.

One fruit seed from knowing to pacing.
Eden. Gethsemane.
Hill at the end of gardens.
A tree found its way to a tree.

*   *   *

I carved on my hill of stockyards
New Tables at storm-core's hush.
How thin now the wailing of Marys,
The meathook nailing of flesh.

Straight hooks were worse, straight lines of road or creed;
My worst gall wasn't gall:
Caliban wasn't Caliban, Prospero was;
Judas wasn't Judas, it was Paul.

I see two midgets in a circus pummel
Each other with rival bladders, Lab or Faith,
While in the bleachers Bacchus, belching
An ode to Arcady, spits grape seeds down on both.

I see their 'good for' or their 'good,'
Their godless joy or joyless God,
While a trampled bouncy 'bad' green weed
Yawns at dry wood.

The only lamb who got away,
I warn the village green:
Don't ride with your Good Humor man;
White's blackness reddens green.

Lean soapboxers hawk me to losers;
Fat bosses pretend I'm a boss.
All rip-offs—and only one Christian,
The one on the cross.

Is it true a tree got Judas?
Earth's rescue cut short by a noose?
Then no one can save you from saviors.
Run for your lives—God is loose.

Judas, Judas, brother dangler:
Two moons in orbit round a planet's grave.
. . . His kiss sold one lamb only.
Millions roast because I'm love.

My Passion, it drained you of passion.
My teardrops, they drained you of sea.
A garden got lost in a garden.
A tree found its way to a tree.

*   *   *

Who flies toward that or this world's love,
Will cry when sun melts feathers.

Whichever tits you'll reach for then,
They were my mother's.

Whole galaxies held out their nests;
I tried each on for size.
When I forgot thee, O earth stain,
I lost my sky in skies.

Stain is what stays when stomped by
Ideology;
Turn back, turn back, Jan Bockelsen;
Weeds yawned at Calvary.

Original Sin—call it salt of the earth.
Corruption—call it loam.
My cross's lumber came handy.
Two crossbars to fence you from home.

I dreamed up hives of angels
With never a hairy bee:
Perfection weeded gardens—
Trees reborn through a tree.

By vampire wood clenched closer,
I—peering closer—see
Sahara amok among gardens,
Trees sucked dry by a tree.

A mountain offered me This World.
I shrank, I said 'unclean.'
. . . I've changed: all's vain but *vanitas*—
Trust no caress that's not obscene.

What slows up sky's
Descending dish?
A sleepy fire
From when you were a fish.

Then, then one stalling flash is
Time, time in reverse:
The last of the terrors, the fourth of the gateways,
The stain that moves the sun and the other stars.

Seed is for vineyards, not crosses.
Eden. Arcady.
. . . Gardens found out about gardens.
Trees smashed to pieces a tree.

* * *

(Scene snaps back to Part Zero, now changed by choices not chosen before.)

PART ZERO
REPLAYED

What is it hinting at, that synthesis of God and goat[1] in the satyr?
—Nietzsche, *The Birth of Tragedy*

I'd believe only in a god who understood how to dance.
—Nietzsche, *Thus Spake Zarathustra*

To dance . . . Satyrically, the tragic foot.
—William Carlos Williams, *Paterson*

CYCLE ONE REPLAYED

Down

—————————

Bromio, sweet Bromio . . . whose muses live.
    —invocation to Dionysus-Bacchus-Bromio
        in Euripides, *The Bacchae*

And Adam called his wife's name Eve;
because she was the mother of all living.
                —Genesis, 3:20

We have given to thee, Adam, no fixed seat. Neither heavenly nor
earthly have We made thee. . . . Thou art . . . the molder and maker
of thyself; thou mayest sculpt thyself into whatever shape thou dost
prefer.
—Giovanni Pico, Prince of Mirandola, the Christian Hebraist
    plus Hellenist, *Oration on the Dignity of Man, 1486*

Place, voice, time: Gethsemane, Son of Man, today. In this new cycle one,
"Down," son is reversing the earlier cycle one, "Up," that opened his earlier
Part Zero; same choice between up-to-sky or down-to-earth. If on stage, slow
pacings keep step with long voice rhythms. Backdrop of Mediterranean
("Midsea"[2] of Eve-Aphrodite and Dionysus).

(Son, alone, is addressing his varying imagined hearers.)

1. (to his Anti-Christ)
Half-brother, Pagliacci-Nietzsche, why do you wrong me so?

Give me your hand, I was always
                    Dionysus-Bromio.
It was good when gods weren't godly and stones not tablet but stone;
Lambs not for nailing but feasting; goat-leaps not symbol but fun.

(to his Dionysus)
When we were doubles, not rivals, two shimmers of southern wine,
You daubed the Midsea into life with the lightheaded light of a vine;
For the painting's in the paintbrush as the dance is in the grape.
Yet dust's a thirsty canvas, a drought green paint can't drape.
And all gods were . . . immortal; all greens were . . . evergreen;
And leaves we trod will tread us on a top the seasons spin.
To punish God for dying, we died and couldn't die;
We sons in orphaned gardens, our crowns went thorny-dry.
Since then, my autumned rival, your light-eyed Arcady
Aches toward the heavy eyelids that weigh Gethsemane.

2. (facing prehistoric painted cave of Dordogne)
Eyes after eyes came feasting on a paint-fleck's inedible deer,
A brush-flick—age after ages—outflinging hunter and spear.
Before the goggles of language partitioned viewer from view,
Here sight—not conned by concept—saw every antler new,
Deer not yet staled to deerhood. On cave walls of Dordogne
Art wasn't art but lifeblood; man's selfsurpass of man
Faced wordlessly in formcraft the gates of birth-spawn-death.
These painted deer, dusk feeds them, they breathe a muskier breath
As if the caves art kindles were life's lost nine-month nest:
O rock my church never built on, arched gate it never blest,
A bloom gardened from bloom dust, doomed flesh affirming 'no.'

(to his would-be disciples and then to his parents)
You 'Christians' who vacuumed me dustless: I'm so much Bromio
I wish I'd deserted from 'love.' O insolent loveliness.
But all you hothouse simperers, soughing so bland a yes,
Are you seedless crystal arbors
                              or Eve's spewed apple pits,
My fellow ethereal spirits?—born when a birth hole shits.
. . . Father, the worst forsaking was not by thee of me,

Me born when a—
                mother, mother, it was me forsaking thee
A little while for a crownlet. O delouse me of purity;
Scour me of God plague, replant me, and bear me all over again.

3. (facing mirror)
And all still ends in questions and starts and ends in pain.
Did I oust or renew Dionysus? In what alley did Paul mug Pan?
When love-touch thinned to love-mist, befogging eye's windowpane,
Palms[3] dried into Palm Sunday; grape's Mass drained grape breasts dry.
Transcenders are but descenders as a spire is lightning-prone,
And no gate saves from dying, but one gate saves from sky.
And still from unknown oceans to exits overknown,
We're tossed; and when we jostle, some turn a wistful eye.

4. (facing Cranach's painting of Eve)
Did the God-book have to slander my loamborn sister so?
Eve was always in secret the foamborn as I was Bromio.
The insolence of her loveliness was a gull cry bitter and wild:
Fig, not figleaf, not 'full of Grace' but Midsea's graceful child,
Eve-Aphrodite, tide's double moon, a Greek and Jew.
Can newfangled monks of the sci lab or old ones of gothic murk
Reduce her to white-smocked Hygeia or the swarthy graffiti of smirk?
A thousand paintings relume her, from cave to canvas to loo,
A phoenix brighter when darker, besmirched and bewinged by a brush,
Till art's but her arson remembered, her Eden re-embered from ash.
You monks once lived in deserts; now deserts live in you;
Lab's drought outdries the church's; the mulch can't slake the parch;—

  (to painting of Eve)
Gate queen, from male's uprootings rescue the tendrils of touch.
Archway, for what are you arching? Umbilic-strung bow of that arch,
Launch us to reach beyond the flesh for beyonds only flesh can reach.

5. (facing cave again)
Launched from a planet's belly, a cave child dreams in stone.
The deer are *in* the paintbrush his scouring tears will hone.

That brush—whatever he aimed for—its flick outflings his aim
And says 'thou canst' to grandsons and says to God 'I am.'

   (you, entering)
"His daubings, aping Creation, got grounded for poaching on God—"
Yet skip to you over time's ocean as light as a skimming shard.

   (you, pointing in consternation as walls suddenly flicker)
"That white, that red! Is he pouring down
Like thawed stalactites from his den
All generations since Dordogne?"—Your tribal dawn.
"My fathers' fathers hurtling home?"—Lava to loam.
"Or runaway paint-streaks, Form undone?"
Or, skimming time's ditch, his
                              signed
                                   stone.
"Arming his grandson's grandsons?" —In the very core of your bone.

6.
"Genes diced him too tipsy a bow grip (the wound of his mutant thumb)."
I was always too skittish a goat leap (miscast in an ox's doom).
"He was always a capering death march." —Toward being who he was.
"Leaving me little to arm with." —Wrenched skull, wrenched artist claws.
"Racked from a finny lungfish?" —Into these hands, this brow.
"Both stretched too taut for gripping. God wins—I'm letting go.
I should've stayed fish; no, fish feel too; I should've stayed numb
Kelp scum. Dead fathers, drown me. Was the selfsurpass worth the grief?"
God only fears one arrow: God's image, made human by Eve.
Now, archer in the marrow, stretch your own birth-cord's bow.

CYCLES TWO AND THREE REPLAYED:

Gods

"Hacked," the earlier cycle two, had ended with the torn Dionysus. "Round," the earlier cycle three, had ended by trapping son in inescapable repetitions. In this replay, the release of both gods from sky depends on man's try at uniting on earth these severed halves.

---

1. (you, then son)
*"A 'god'—the word is old hat—today means
What?"* —A leaping dolphin of delight.
Or leaping electron-quantum. All that shimmers

Uncomputably. —*"A nuisance imp to programs?"*
A bursting grape of spontaneity.
"Spontaneity—will it blast or heal?"
Heals you of mek. Then blasts you, too,
Unless you garden it.
"Shedding the chains of programmings, why
Not also of form?
Full speed ahead for the pure of heart, unbound.
Or does 'gardened' mean: no more green mass?"
More and sproutier. But green-gone-formless ends as
Youth drugged with truth-
Slogans. Heart's open-road from oh-wow to *Sieg Heil.*

    (you, then son: *Straighteners*)
"Progress! Ah, pruned by Euclid's tome?"
Poor logic-sharp Procrustes: no green thumb.
"Straight lines are the shortest distance between two points."
Straight lines are the bloodiest distance between blueprints.

"How launch a lib no blood can warp?"
Smite Goliath with David's . . . harp.
"What slave-freeing stone enslaved the slave?"
Baby Goliath's, when his name was . . . Dave.

"Revolution?"—Catnip for halfgods
Shedding Papa Doc's 'ancien régime.'
"To be whole, not half, what more must we shed?"
Mom. Hear my Christ-of-the-barricades dream:—

    (son: *REVOLUTION, Each Halfgod's Dream;* striding
    back and forth, son paces these short lines with
    ominous slowness—yet ever more nervously)
God sowed me too down under.
I waited three dense days.
Compressing all the loneness
Returners face,
My sprouting stare cracked stone as if
My scars were maize.

Piero della Francesca,
Painting my exhumed gaze,
Guessed what—for resurrection—
The resurrected pays:
How lewdly, as if meat were grass,
Tombs graze on loins' embrace;
How cold on eyeballs the earthball
Weighs.
The Easter I never asked for
(Dank from that airless space)
Across my opening eyelids
Now seasonally lays
A slither of snails no Easter lace,
No lily sprigs, no incense sprays
Efface.

                    *   *   *

What corpse was fool enough to rise
For some half-simian race?
Each Easter rakes the bedsores in
My snowtime doze and daze.
And when the March alarm clock frays
My sleep and waylays and betrays,
I'd still not cheat clenched tombs nor raise
Lids. But my skull—twixt worms and words—
Twirls livelier than life
                    and slays
The death I should have died.
From globe's volcanic carapace,
Love, is it love, erupting me
Up through rock and back through clay's
Lock
        (from the grave I'm asking this)
Or is my crown my craze?

                    *   *   *

Once God made ash of Eden
With his 'loving' guardian-rays;
Returners are accusers;

Returners are ash
                yet blaze.
Eyes of forsaken sons
Deface
         erase erase
Walls. Wistfulness
Leaves none in place.
No forts, no jails: where rebel brows
Stub against stone, they raze.
Orphans of living fathers,
Echoes no cave replays,
Tunesters whose crowns of bays
Are fool's-caps, thorns as bells:
We cindered yesterdays,
Can we retrace decay's
Arc in reverse,
                we green
Ashes of grays?
We launch our embering eye-coals at
God's Sistine Chapel face.
At his stone stare; at his dome-arch brow;
At his lackey-groomed patriarch grace.
Then why the wink of complicity
From the ceiling the tourists praise?
(As if father and son were trapped as one
In a mirror maze.)
And now lean back, my earthmom;
I must lie on you face to face
To guard you (from lustful dustlings)
With my truly loving rays.
. . . Ah truth (how tell essence from incense?):
Now perfume cleans truth's haze
Of carrion-stench from nails below;
We sons adore my modest ways
And groom my grace.
Freedom's enforced; each tombstone stays
Sealed; all's in place.
. . . What's this in my fortress mirrors?

Quick, lackeys, crack their glaze.
Why does my lying traitor-glass
Show father's Sistine face?

*   *   *

    (you, then son)
"Enough of pendulums. What midpoint stays?"
A kingdom. Of this world. The wine-dark Middle Sea's.
Not mine yet. Yours no longer.
"Dead classics? Schliemann moles still digging?"
In your own skull nine-egos-deep[1] lives Greece.
"Greece not in Greece now?" —Nor in still-born reprints.
What's most alive and far-away and smallest
Hides in whatever's your big new nearest town.

    (you: *Small Perfect Manhattan*)
"Unable to breathe, I inhaled the classic Aegean.
Losing my northern shadow, I sheared the noon
Of an almond grove. The tears of marble
Thanked me for laughter.

Shapes! And 'release, release' rustled the quarries;
'One touch will free the serenity locked in our stones.'
But archipelagoes of olives
Distracted me shorewards,

Where sails were ripening toward an African sleep.
That sirocco was no friend of the wind of harps.
Not destiny but destination
Incited the grain ships.

'Nevertheless be of cheer,' said a jolly skipper;
'I sell sick goats that once were deft at flutes.
The lizard who now is proconsul of Carthage
Will bury you sweetly.'

But No to sweet Charon. Then home—then not to Sahara,
The elephants'-graveyard of classics—ascended the singing

Green I wove just the size of the brow of
Small perfect Manhattan."

* * *

(son)

You're almost half-ready for her who sleeps inside you.
        (Aphrodite wraith rises from your eyes as you close
        them. Slow music; exit son. You to Aphrodite:)

"Intangible bodiless spirit,
Are you part of my One far God?"

(Aphrodite to you)

To wraiths we appear as wraiths;
Our bodies, near and disguised,
Are warming you here and now.
God? No, but gods! —who'd strip for mere abstract ones?
Obscenely shrine, piously desecrate us,
Our swelling fruit half terror, half decorum,
Flesh flushed with spilling wine: we touchable gods.

(you gawking at her, while blue ceiling shakes and cracks)
        "The times of her pulse shake blue
        Glassfuls of sky. Two gulls
        Scream vowels in her wake:
        Lone longings pair like chimes.

        "The way her sinews move
        (Each tilt, each groove a moon's
        Lasso to tides) has spilt
        Sky —the way tunes crack glass

        With shy internal rhymes.

(Aphrodite to you)

Viewed voyeur, have you really looked close at what my opening
Opens? A wound to heal wounds. Salt
To sweeten salt.

A crescent moon of berserk gentleness, parting
A full moon. Shimmer of inner.
. . . I still am I, the mussed up goddess.
What I've returned to bring is not salvation—
Too much of that too long too many eons—
But choice between God and gods.
Here comes a cypress jury-grove to judge
Your backtalk to the southwind. You have made
The Fig cloacal and the Fountain chemic,[2]
Whereby your sky's first constellation crashed.
For this the courts of Eros sentence you
To health
    and to drum majorettes
        and to
Street smartness when awkward awe is overdue.

 (Aphrodite, now more somber-voiced, then you: *Stabat Mater*)
My park was parched by her desert eyes,
By the tug-past-death of Mary's eyes,
Twice beautiful, with birth and then with heartbreak,
With a lapful of life and then with world's weightiest death—first
The piety, then the *Pietá*—she
Standing there twice with Burden in her arms.
For this (though she banned me) I twice kissed the ground
(Though sullenly) where she stood.
   "You, once our bewitcher—"
Now your witch;
My mud crown crueler than his thorns. Don't judge
My Olympus by underground Venusberg.
   "No overground queendom?"
Soon, soon, when my beauty and Mary's
Crisscross with equal pride.
   "Meanwhile your hide-out was—?"
The other Mary.
Till she lost him. Next day I went underground.

 (Backdrop of oldfashioned music hall; Aphrodite as the Magdalen, "the other Mary," banging offkey harmonium and shifting to singsong ballad voice:)

What's Venus up to anyhow
Now that her doves are crows?
I'm playing 'The Ballad of Maggie Jones,'
And here is how it goes.

I don't much like humanity;
My love is lilt, not vow;
It's not mankind I'm warming but
A near one, here and now.

It's me, repenting repentance,
You hear when a mattress groans.
What goddess haunts the downstairs couch
Whenever Smith dates Jones?

Whether I give you lust or birth,
You all crawl out and cry.
I tuck you back, you still won't stay
In any womb but sky.

My love needs dollars, God's needs souls;
Mine is the cheaper fee.
My quicksand hugs for half a night,
His for eternity.

I've nothing at all to heal the sick
Except myself to share,
My few warm inches of cosiness
Against his acres of air.

So what could I do but join his troupe?
His magic seemed stronger than mine—
Till Smith's boy Judas rang my bell,
More drunk with the bread than the wine.

Young Judas kissed my breasts and said,
'Eternity's too old.

I hate a sky I cannot touch.
I hate God's love; it's cold.'

*   *   *

(Eerie pipings. Wraith of tiny furry FAUN rises from you and chants
   to you)
I, lowliest godlet, scorn your highest, who've
No time for time.
Bloom is serene explosion; you blast the slow
Unfold of things.
Impertinence of leaves to root:
The fact that you're so many of you
Is smirk for plague's macabre dance to cure.
From goats that gods in heat have rubbed against,
From noon-struck thickets horned with shaggy hints,
An ancientness of pipings laughs at you.
You geld your satyrs or glut them; twice wrong; —attune!
Face, face and hug your formless shivering chaos
Warm into form, Ionia's
strict wild dance.
Gardening their wishes, terrace over terrace,
Our vineyard children knew: what counts is levels.
Your lusts—don't dare call them lusty—they're but snigger.
Poison for you: the wine without the wine-god,
Our naked freedom without our
formal dance.

(you to faun but pointing to Aphrodite:)
"Form, form—I hate it—your uptight pond,
What miracle made it her ocean?"

(Aphrodite huddles against painted ocean backdrop. Faun, beside her,
   to you: *The Ripple at Cythera*)
Blue silence. Thickening. Then the long slow ripple.
The waves lobbed one shared language at the headlands.
Who'd guess a girl-child's relevance to harvests?
Yet the nudged beach quivered

A consternation of tiptoe herons;
Though dawn still was pallid,
Wind swayed a wheatfield of wakening nipples.
And from the shorelines up the dunes, a rumor:
'With muffled fins a saboteur has landed.'
But no, not fins; only a calcified Oh,
A nothing, a housed echo. Who'd guess pulse there?
The first boy who pocketed the first
Sea shell, knapsack of wounds,
Was smuggling inland the singing birthpangs,
Staining the dry hills with droned foam.
Calamitous blessing,
What sterner sweetness once walked a loveless earth?
Do elms hoard reveries from feverless ages
Before that flabbergasting lilt was born?
No land-sound but was changed forever after,
Rubbing with a new reverberation
The sheens of bloom, the taffetas of wind,—
Riddling the rhythms of the works of man
With added resonance of
Undertow.

        (you: mortal's *Invocation to Aphrodite*)
   "*Undertow,*
   You other blue,
   Tow us to you.
   Came sky; in upside-down of sky, there loured
   Undertow.
   Came Greek year; form held only what a port can
   Of undertow.
   Came Gothic year and Abelard gored; yet somewhere
   Lurked undertow.
   Rococo came, pink pudge depilatoried;
   Yet undertow.
   Queened, demoned, pseudo-tamed, renamed, there always
   Was undertow.
   Lines of the straighteners, grids of nerves and subways,

Are coming; indestructible below
Is undertow.
Us, goddess, too,
Swerve not too late from where we hurtle to;
Sway up unearned—for us who earn the arson—
The olive[3] *too."*

(Austerely, uncoyly, Aphrodite speaks counter-invocation to mort
Last Day of Childhood)
Too long with unvoluptuous Hygeia,
You need my luring, my tellurian yawn.
Not up but down, down, earthward is your sky,
Your own (but how to make you know?) by birth.
There shines the park that offers you more lilacs
Than all the arms of longing can enfold.
And so you grow, you grope for parks while drifting
All the while southward all unknowingly.
Then groves more south, more slow than lukewarm breezes
(More south, more velvet) sing you dissonances
(More dense, more south) that cloy unbearably,
Till every vibrant, swaying twig bends down
Heavy with fig and with the breasts of vine.

Such exhalation, then, of tenderness—
Of fondling tides on crumbling promontories,
Of shade of clouds on white young birch-bark, fleeting
As patterns hinted on the wildest grasses
By rims of bicycles in picnic weather—
Slakes you to sleepiness. You snuff the sun out;
You unroll far beaches to your chin like quilts.
You become a *Märchen* dreamed by the deep, cool clams
And by the huddling bats of timeless caves.
Two thousand years of this. And then a signal.
You'll know, you'll never doubt it, you'll arise;
And, yawning, stretch into a constellation;
And fill my sky that has been waiting for you.

(Aphrodite and faun vanish. You alone, still partly under their
god-spell:)
"Christ's lips are dry; my sweet wine slakes them wet.
Pan's eyes are dry; my tear-salt aches them wet.
A god can learn from a man;
Half knows only half:
Tears and compassionate pain
Or carousal and passionate laugh."

    (son, re-entering, then you)
None but your saltsweet earth-race grows
From strict brows
                wild goat-grace.
"Will it storm us the heavenly city?"
When the village below binds fast
A Pan who finds out about pity
And a Jew-god drunk at last.
"Each flawed alone?" —Myself too sober-paced.
"Then why not rites of spring? Fauns giddy-faced?"
In statues grand, in life a bit inane.
"Too frisky?" —Fluffed. No ballast of human-scale pain.
"What makes two rival god-lies true for us?"
Crisscross.
    (son echoes Dionysus lines from cycle two)
If—one son torn, One nailed—our brotherly war ends,
Unsnarling burrs of dogma from our garlands,
If east and East reverse west's icy rout,
Father, watch out.
We whelps of God: a mulch for spring's
Jack-in-the-box, we're ladderlessly chained
Below. But what when we two, blending, bend
Chains into rungs?
"I said, 'I must duel near water'—'water,' I, earthling, called.
I said, 'I feel salt stinging'—the brine in me yanked by the salt."
The showdown with the Showman must end where the show began:
Land's End again.
"But what can I win there?" —You're now on your own,
My errand done.

"Far sea mist. Thickening nearer. How face Land's End
Without you?" —DON'T RUN. Stand
Where first you landed with fraying fins,
Gasping for breath ever since.
"The blue too gray, the wind too wet."
Just right for showdown at shoreline.
"No gods to the rescue?" —The loving ones chain you with love.
And now goodbye at the edge you were always at. —*"Wait!*
What's left of lamb-goat crisscross if you shake
Me off?"
When the great contraries claim you, take
Over. Twine.

(Son, hereafter unheard from, vanishes through side curtain. Enter angry
father, jarred from sleep and wearing old dressing gown of frayed constel-
lations.)
Earsplitting binge downstairs; some wise-guy
Hollering up—and at this late hour—'old Lizard Eye.'
What half-assed joke, what half-brained—
"Half-selved. But when my lost self gets regained
And 'meddler' need meddle no more and I'm on my own—"
From a god who's a dartboard, what can you gain?
"The one nailed carpenter made all nails vain."

(father with arms outstretched toward side curtain)
Sky child, for man's sake traitor, changeling son:
Sharing all the world's burdens, how could you forget
Mine?— the stern must-it-be-yes-it-must
That gnaws my grin the way my red gnaws green.
Almost I envy dust each groan
It shares between gate and gate.

(you facing same empty side curtain)
"Was my clown-lamb spirit or gut?
I heard a sea shell hum
That is takes a sea queen strolling home
To make dust loam, to make lamb goat.
Or was it Eve strolled by my door last week,

Spitting apple pits? —new orchards in her wake.
Jericho falls when a four-beat waltz—"
Not quite. It's time for our seaside walks.

(Regaining control, father now confidently replays the opening "Show-down on Land's End." Same sign: ALLHALLOWS EVE; same bleak sea-side meadow. Same and not same; spiral.)
"Tunes warmer on winds waywarder than others
When from the frozen graves the marshfires glow,
Bring me—." —A three-step from your fathers' fathers.
Against them, you need what I've lent you, your armor of snow.
"Snow round my heart? Snow against rain?"
My winter protects; grow is foe.
"Maybe we two are the foes. Having. It. Out. On
Land's End." —Land's start. Where my million-year showdown with man
Began. . . . Time to end. Your tombed fathers—
"Fathers no more, my faced selves now"—
Are melting your armor—/—*"that now I don't need."*
Without it, seed grows—/—*"already the meadow less yellow"—*
Grows amok in the end.
"This time, green's not formless but gardened.
And when, tomorrow, vine's garland—"
These Bacchic spooks you follow, mists they borrow,
Are Rorschach blurs to tease forth selves you bury.
They're Hallowe'en tricksters to harry you; run from the meadow.
"Claws below; breaking through." —RUN; wildness is loose;
Why are you standing? —*"Loose? Wildness is freed*
To serve
      form's strictest
            offbeat."
Whose?

(Enter vine-wreathed Asian stranger of cycle two, the "Hacked" cycle. Father and you stare at him through meadow mist.)
Look: who's that dancing . . . kicking dust at sky?
"Here—last time—a gull watched the meadow."
I see . . . odd . . . footprints. —*"Yet gestures of my village."*
He gibbers odd tongues. —*"Yet accents of my village."*

Who knows him? —*"Known in my marrow."*
No dreamscape of classic myth. Look up: real jets.
"Look down: Jerusalem's palms, strewn for a leopard-pulled cart."
Mice on a wheelbarrow. —*"If it's mirage,*
Is Land's End right under my village?"
   (each mumbling aloof:)
If it's me that halluci . . . then almost—
"Now two of him, one pale, one noon-flushed"—
Then gut-string's bow could almost launch an arrow.
"Two shapes—no, one shape—kicking . . . loam at sky."
Warmed lifelike by her who came home, he's only your shadow.
"A shadow that sweats?"
Well, then he's only—/—*"I see"*—
Some local wino—/—*"I see*
Hacked hands; no, pierced—"/—no, mere vine twigs.
"Pierced hands . . . bending cross into crossbow.
Look: goatfoot Jesus on the village green."

(CURTAIN)

Epilogue

(PROLOGUE TO NEW SPIRAL)

In front of final descended curtain, father assigns paintbrushes to you and himself, removes paintings ("Slaughtered Ox," "Adoration of Lamb") of "Motifs" and sets up blank canvas.

(you, casually hanging your cap on ceiling meathook)
"Toys don't know they're toys.
Now that we do, we're not.
A thing and not a thing.
A circle and a dot."

(father, turning his back on you and facing audience with bored voice of an old pro)
Somebody had to keep the show on the road.
Am I accountable to stage-props? Tell your Lamb
All rounds are simultaneous to sky and
Down. I am that I am.[1]

APPENDIX:

Form in Poetry:

Would Jacob Wrestle with a Flabby Angel?

———————

I will not let thee go, except thou bless me.
—Jacob wrestling with the
angel of God's "form," Genesis 32:26

*It don't mean a thing
If it ain't got that swing.*
—Duke Ellington, 1931

I. BIOLOGY—THE SCANNER SCANNED

Is poetry in English still a continuity? A shared continuity? Does it
have a structure not mechanical but alive, with strict motions of muscle and torso that are not private contortions but a general language,
a shared yet nonverbal language? If the answer to these questions is,
as here assumed, yes, then why is the assumption not widely shared?
Why do many writers and readers today answer these questions with
no? Something is wrong when the self-evident isn't evident, even to
the most thoughtful and sensitive readers of poetry.

Nor is it sufficient to note that tradition is *vieux jeu* in an age of
rebel panache; the language of poetry depends on physical rhythms far
too concrete to be budged by the abstractions of either revolution or
reaction. The difficulty lies in the fact that, unlike other languages,
poetic rhythms speak on two levels instead of one. Worse still: the
two levels tend to contradict each other. All verse (even the purest

lyric) is thereby verse-drama, a duel. All rhythms, being at war with each other, are sword-rhythms. The actionless dramatic-action of poetic language is not physical acts or verbal acts, but physical waves of rhythms and their delicate or pounding counterspray.

A broader question: Has our response to poetry (our real response, not official response) been less to meaning-plus-sound than to meaning-versus-sound? Obviously both kinds of response are essential; though here I happen to be discussing the secret rhythm-connotations, I would never intend to undermine the equal need for overt word-denotations: the need for defending the dignity of ideas against romantic anti-intellectualism. The intention, rather, is to admit that we know less about our own language than about distant stars—and to concentrate an inward telescope on the non-word language of rhythm. When the non-word language contradicts the word-messages, it does so to enrich, not to replace, them. Both kinds of language are not only needed; they fulfill each other, and thus bespeak the familiar dialectics of growth-through-contradiction.

Still, the differences are there. A word-message is indicative or imperative in grammar; it is, at least partly, conscious; and is relatively loose in formal construction. A rhythm-message is conditional or subjunctive in grammar; it is at least partially unaware; and requires the strict forms evolved over many centuries of a shared poetry experience. The allocation of brain functions between left and right hemispheres is still speculative, but let us at least speculate whether the biological basis for the difference between the word message of denotative prose and the rhythm message of connotative verse is that the former belongs more to the left hemisphere and the latter to the right.

In 1975 a sensitive Shakespearean director summed up his career in one provocative sentence: "Meter is the real key to understanding Shakespeare." But in view of the tension between Shakespeare's Apollonian surface pentameters and his Dionysian subsurface tetrameters and trimeters,[1] the "key to understanding" him is not so much meter as meter-clash. This continues to be a key to prosody today.

Poetry does not write about what it writes about. Most critics agree that poetry, more than scientific or scholarly prose, leaves a gap between statement and implication, the latter the "real" meaning. Is the gap caused by two levels of diction (in part our heritage from the French *symbolistes*)? Or is that gap more innately inherent, as here suggested, in two levels of rhythm? The diction explicators have brought us to a blind alley by being oversubtle about the ambiguities and ambivalences of diction and undersubtle about those of rhythm. The fact that good prose (not to mention purple "poetic" prose) also has two rhythm-levels is not to the point. The tension between two irregular rhythms, as in prose, is simply not the same as that between one irregularity and one formal, traditionally shared regularity in poetry.

The half-conscious uncovering of rhythm's hidden language helps explain an ancient truth: unlike a prose essay, a tragic poem or a tragic *verse*-play may leave the reader feeling exalted while an exalting love poem may leave him mournful. The explanation is not some miraculous "transcending" of tragedy and of the human condition (as if the presumptuous poet were doing God's work for Him better) but the uncovering of a palimpsest layer. What will be needed, from now on, are not generalizations (like this one) but precise trochee-by-iamb-by-spondee analyses of why the relevant passages in *King Lear*, for example, achieve tragic joy by means of the joy-connoting rhythms beneath the somber words. While translating certain German and Russian poets of our century, I am attempting such an analysis in parallel languages. Maxim: the translator should consult his dictionary less and his ear more (searching not for lilt duplications by metronome but for lilt equivalents by connotation). Poets, then, are not our Shelleyan "unacknowledged legislators" but our unacknowledged kinaesthesia.

At one time the columns of Bernini "made marble speak." Today the rhythms of the lyric are the onomatopoeia of the flesh. As the dance language of bees is (to us) both cryptic and informative, so will our rhymed and metrical love lyric be seen in the future as earth's earthiest, nuttiest, and most practical artifact. It is not a flight from reality. Reality flees from it. And thereby to it? Either way, metrics inspire motion. Flesh feels a poem's beauty not as picture but motion. Metronomes can't feel; the motion they tick is not gesture but tic. Motion is a duel and not one kind of scansion but two because all poetry is a pun straddling a charade.

Both the scansions here contrasted are accentual. Deliberately omitted is the furtive osmosing of classical quantitative scansions into English. This is not omitted because the counterpull of this third layer of the palimpsest is minor (it becomes major in the sensuous effect of slow-voweled lines with voiced consonants) but because, in the present context, it is a distractingly mine-strewn terrain, where critics rush in with maps too neat to work and poets fear to tread.

Rarely found in the denotational dictionaries of Webster or Euclid and compressed—like some coiled spring—into an explosive core by strict form, the connotations of accentual rhythm are a universal and not just private cryptography; otherwise how can poetry possibly "work"? Poetry that works is too unique for paraphrase (this truth is by now humdrum). But why can't it be paraphrased? Surely its uniqueness is not visual and is not semantic (that is, not simply a matter of image, metaphor, destiny, irony, rhetoric, black humor, original sin, unoriginal virtue, or the rest of the official explicator apparatus; all these visual or else semantic aspects can indeed be paraphrased in unrhythmic prose). Poetry's unparaphrasable uniqueness lies, rather, in its being our unverbalizable pulse; you are not only scanning the poem, the poem is also scanning you.[2]

Spirit is not being subordinated to matter (the question of which came first is left wide open) by a parallel between our bodily nature and the seeming unnaturalness of strict form. Rhythm for sure and probably also rhyme (or its equivalents in echo-pairing: assonance, alliteration, refrain, leitmotif) are not luxury but necessity, not stale or arbitrary conformity but our very anatomy. Free verse and unstrict form are stillborn: not because they are "free" or lack a tennis net but because they lack the recurrences of living flesh. So, at the other extreme, does the dead metronome of the mechanical formalists. What is life, what is poetry, but an organic recurrent vibration?

Without recurrence, no resonance. A "good ear" means or ought to mean a just scale; it balances a background of strict recurrence against a foreground of free change. Rhythm includes not only the official metrics of the schoolma'ams but the unofficial crosscurrent of shifting mood pace, runaway vision, all kinds of prankish onomatopoeias, and the sleepy epiphanies of the caesura. If weighed on the other side of the same just scale, change would not be occurring without the background of regularity that defines it and gives it something to strain against. The stricter the form, the more it downright insists on irregularities (and then assimilates them). It is free verse that soon becomes too regular: the old-fashioned regularity known as prose.

Not the prose writer but the formal poet is marshaling words the way the body organizes its nervous system. Ponder the nervous system's physical structure, its facilitatory and inhibitory signals of reflex conduction, its ballad style refrains, its rhyme style telegrams of reinforcement, the enjambmentlike junctures of its "synapses," and, above all, its farflung contrapuntal controls, ever balancing the terrifying risks and rewards of exposed nerve ends in the world of chaos. This whole neural gestalt is not so much a line of alternating beats as an entire iambic stanza. Both the stanza and the gray matter are coordinating separate "lines" of varying length and of contradictory impulse; they do so by laws of pattern. In contrast, formless verse obeys no law except Gresham's. It is the strictness of form that blesses; would Jacob wrestle with a flabby angel?

Whether our biological pendulum (the thump-THUMP of artery and lung) is but the spilt iambic of a song, or vice versa: either way, biology and poetry are welded by the same scannable tide. The welding not only throws new light on the odd, obsessive quality of poetry's magic; it reestablishes, in the teeth of current opinion, the dependence of that magic on the continuity of traditional meters and even of rhymes.

Is there some inherent link between rhyme and meter, or am I smuggling rhyme in arbitrarily? Rhymes inhere as the punctuation marks of rhythm and therein lies the link. Rhymes are rhythm's brittle-consonanted commas or else its italics, heavy and long-voweled. Rhythm has no need for those metallic rhymes that are a mere stapling machine for two end words: click-click. What rhythm does need is the organic rhymes that we may define as a torrent of mood-signaling vowels, interweaving not two words or two lines but whole symphonies of stanzas. Not merely form but strict form is needed in order to harmonize the runaway autonomy of the separate lines. What, in free verse, is left to hold the lines together? Gesticulating frantically their primadonna solos, they require the conductor's baton of the stanza. Ever since the influence of the success of *The Waste Land,* fragmentation has been justified as mirroring (but why should it mirror?) the momentary social reality. What such fragmentation fails to mirror is the lasting biological reality; here the whole is not sacrificed to the part.

But here, in turn, enters a second kind of fragmentation, a profounder split, not of whole versus parts this time but of conflicting ciphermessages within two simultaneous wholes. How better can the inherent schizophrenias of "civilization and its discontents" be expressed today than by an aesthetic that conveys a surface mood through the literal meaning of the words and a hidden mood through their suggestiveness? For example, my "To Helen" lyric contains a double message: the denotative surface rhythms tell us—with a grammatical error in every line—that this is a comic poem about a gross, crude, pathetic adolescent; the deeper connotative rhythms are trying to hint, in contrast, at the wistful, delicate dignity of all wounded love.

TO HELEN (OF TROY, N.Y.)

I sit here with the wind is in my hair;
I huddle like the sun is in my eyes;
I am (I wished you'd contact me) alone.

A fat lot you'd wear crape if I was dead.
It figures, who I heard there when I phoned you;
It figures, when I came there, who has went.

Dogs laugh at me, folks bark at me since then;
"She is," they say, "no better than she ought to;"
I love you irregardless how they talk.

You should of done it (which it is no crime)
With me you should of done it, what they say.
I wait here with the wind is in my hair.

Call the widening ripples (the rings of connotations around the dropped stone of denotation) illogical or call them psychological; either way, they can voice more of schizophrenia's terror and beauty than can rhymelessness, because the rhyme-ripples possess more codes of communication, more consonant-crescendos, vowel-nudges, and a whole repertoire of semaphore. One such full-throated rhyme-echo, cutting across a whole brisk flurry of later grace-note rhymes, works as a sustaining pedal under the piano keys of, say, ottava rima or of pantoum. Rhyme is the most effective sympathetic magic yet devised for undamming the contradictory Niagaras of the pent-up heart.

Your choice of rhyme scheme sets off not only your collective culture (Shakespearean versus Petrarchan sonnets are setting off Elizabethan versus Florentine Renaissance); your choice also conveys your individual faith. This is as true today as when terza rima was voicing

Dante's Trinitarian Christianity. The particular rhyme pattern you choose is the cookie form you squash down upon the otherwise shape-less dough of thought and feeling. React physically, with tendon and sinew, to rhyme's austere "ah" or lush "u," its mellow or its raging timbres of "o" or "i."[3] Listen (as you would to water under ice) to the undercurrent hauntings of earlier voiced consonants beneath later unvoiced ones.

From centuries of cultural continuity, readers learned form's con-notations unwittingly, often more so when these readers deny the con-tinuity and the sign language. Why all the more so? Because your tidal ear continues to hear these same ebbs and flows that your willed ear has discarded. Borges confessed in 1969: "I once strove after the vast breath of the psalms and of Walt Whitman; after these many years I find (not without a certain sadness) that in all my attempts at free verse I have often gone from one classical meter to another . . ."

Today these "discarded" old forms are still molding you. They act on you "like wine during animated conversation" (Coleridge). Form-rejectors like William Carlos Williams ("We are through with the iambic pentameter . . . the measured quatrain") are often excessive formalists deep down: crushed by their own "unnoticed" metric tick-tock, they can function only by pretending (to themselves) to be deaf to it. But without it, they would have nothing to be formless *against.* Their parasitic art would die if they really did succeed in killing their host instead of merely driving him underground. Underground can be a very snug place to be. The taut, nervous rhythms of Hopkins and old Yeats first excited us because, like Hopkins and old Yeats himself, we kept hearing—underground—the contrast with the younger Yeats and with Tennyson.

But will there come a day when nobody reading Williams hears the contrasting undercurrents? More than one such major writer has pro-claimed the death of rhyme and even of iambics. Why have these artifices always returned to bury the burier? Because they are not artif-ices. Because, when organic, they *are* that same free naturalness which free verse merely articulates but form incarnates. It is formal verse which is free and natural. "I wish to write such rhymes," said Emer-son, "as shall not suggest a restraint but contrariwise the wildest free-dom." List at random the natural functions of your own anatomy, and what do they turn out to be? Inhale and exhale of breath, systole and diastole of heart, pound and pause of pulse, in and out of coition, ebb and flow of tide: all are iambics. Iambics are throbbing the alternating currents of electric shock as well as the heroic couplet contractions of paired sphincters. It is for these biological reasons that iambics always will be the basic beat of organic poetry. What are trochees but iambics in reverse? What are dactyls and anapests but iambics with stutter?

Why, one gets asked in poetry "workshops," why isn't it just as natural for poems to scan every which way as to move along on alternate beats? The condign reply is a counterquestion: Do human beings move like amoebas, on pseudopods every which way, or on two feet with alternate steps?

Nothing is imprinted deeper on the nervous system of every embryo than the alternating pulse of the mother, first as womb beat and then as heartbeat, and this at a rate of some 100 beats per minute, the tempo later found most attractive in music.[4] Is this the ultimate source of man's impulse to pound out scansion? Such pound-pound-pounding is often ridiculed as crude and naive. Students are made ashamed of writing with lilt or responding corporeally to the boomlay-boom of the underrated Vachel Lindsay.

According to a recent study in *Scientific American,* human mothers instinctively—determined by genes?— hold their babies to their left (heart) side. So do the madonnas of Renaissance paintings. When babies grow up, their voice rhythms continue to be iambic, as Aristotle already noted. In fact, there is a book devoted entirely to the impact of this trait on civilization; William Calvin, author of *The Throwing Madonna* (New York, 1983), is a feminist and neurophysiologist.

In no way need these biological verities play into the hands of a body-cult think-with-blood romanticism. Mind—the artist's conscious rational craftsmanship—is the indispensable supplement to these biological verities. The laborious revisions of Blake, Keats, and Yeats show the cold intellectual crafts of the most inspired, most warmth-evoking lyricists. As bartenders, they serve their intoxicating brew by staying classically sober; their austere intellects are needed to canalize across to us their emotional ecstasy. Thereby they form—through form—the subjective and personal into the objective and universal.

* * *

Is it coincidence that the "foot" you walk on is also the name of the scansion unit? We don't walk camera-style on tripods. A biped's iambs and trochees are more basic than anapests and dactyls. Even though every reader can cite famous anapest poems of gallop and rush, their mimesis—too contrivedly functional—is more stunt than centrally human; who cares how Browning got those damned quadrupeds from Aix to Ghent?

Iambs and trochees are what mathematics calls a binary code. The two-beat rhythm—and by analogy the two-click rhyme—are coding and condensing our multinumbered reality. The imagination fishes in our semiconscious (a more accurate term in poetry than unconscious) for the matching multilevels of free-association released by binary rhythm and binary rhyme. The stricter the form, the freer is this free-association. What infinite variety of undertow may inhere in the alleged monotony of two alternating steps!

Yet it would oversimplify to see biological roots solely in the two-syllable foot. That would ignore the mysteriously compelling intensity of anapests interspersed among iambs. If iambs are the pulse of an isolated physiology, anapests are sometimes the interacting different-tempo'd pulsations of two bodies intensely conjoined, as in love or combat. Consider, for example, the carnal onomatopoeia of what is rhythmically the strongest line in all Kipling, a Swinburnian anapest-iamb mix: "That the sin they do by two and two they must pay for one by one." Still, we happen to have only two feet, two pings of heart pulse, two breath-alternates.

In rethinking postmodern form, two groups, psychoanalysts and Marxists, believe they know enough to explain, for example, my opening observation about the frequent conflict between word-denotations and rhythm-connotations. Freudian critics "know" the rival messages are social-parental restraint versus underground desire. Except for its reductiveness, this explanation was superbly illuminating for a certain kind of inhibited society. Less so today, when, in confessional poetry, the id sexuality has surfaced and the repressed spirituality is the dirty secret. Meanwhile Marxists "know" that the same two levels represent a class-based superstructure versus repressed economic reality. Yet, the unknowable Proteus is still eluding the rival Procrusteans of System.

The dead formalism of the metronome gives equal weight to all accented words or syllables. But in living form, there are occasions when the real alternative to "accented" is not "unaccented" but "still more accented." This occasional "still more" can make or break a poem;

it can either intensify or disintegrate the strictness of form. What it may be signaling is a sudden exciting unevenness in the imperceptible body tremors that accompany, follow or precede the competing accents. This merely physical overstress of accent becomes—in the magic code-language of strict form—an intellectual or moral overstress. It gives certain accented words more urgency than other accented words, even though the latter may carry the very different "official" intention and would win the conflict if scanned in equal metronome fashion. Like Orwell's pigs, some accents are more equal than others. This sabotage is usually done (hinted at) by the writer. It can also be done by the readers. German factory workers, forced to sing (that is, scan) Nazi songs, sometimes reversed the meaning—not necessarily on purpose or they would have been shot—by slightly overaccenting such words as "red" (for example, in flag colors).

After tempest, music. Not all conflict can or ought to be resolved. But much great art does end with an all-inclusive resolving chord, a Shakespearean reconciliation of the varied conflicts in word meanings, muscle rhythms, and accents. Why does the reconciling chord have such a compelling force when in "real life" it is the tempest that has more energy? Better ask: Why does a vibrating bridge give way to the resonance of soldiers in step? Our nerve-synapse bridges, with their workaday resistance to rapt reconciliation, give way to the accumulated resonance of an art that is in step. They do not give way to that formless amble, the artlessness that conceals artlessness.

In his 1942 Glasgow lecture, Eliot observed (in a cautious echo of Yeats) that a poem "may realize itself first as a particular rhythm before it reaches expression in words." Yes indeed, but why is there this Eliotine reticence about the body? In other words, why stop at the second link of the three-link chain of word, poem rhythm, body rhythm? Today "heartthrob" gets taken not literally but as metaphor. Throbs of heart and body are quite literally one of the origins of strict form in poetry; and when the throbs are uneven, they are one of the origins of our revolt against the dead formalist kind of strictness.

My phrase, "one of the origins," leaves open the possibility of non-bodily origins of form. The three-link causal chain may also work in reverse, beginning not with the subliminal body throb but with the conscious word—or even the spiritual Word. On an earlier page Dante's terza rima was seen as the physical shadow of his spiritual Trinity.

Strict form, in the broadest sense of "form," may be both creator and product of the entire immortal macrocosm (as well as of the microcosmic mortal poem). The causal chain may not only be running either way alternatively but—as a third explanation—may interact both ways simultaneously.

Body language includes the way our senses are triggered by certain consonants, especially when made more resonant by rhyme. *Re* smell: consider the nasal "sn" of such sniffing words as snoot, snort, sneeze, snuff, snore, snout, snivel. Hence the both snotty and snoopy connotations of Faulkner's Snopes family. *Re* taste: consider the reflexes— the mouth watering, the tongue savoring—induced by Keat's "lucent syrops, tinct with cinnamon." *Re* the baby's suckling of its mother's milk: this lip reflex is triggered by the letter "m," the first letter of most Indo-European words for milk and mother.

2. A STRICTER RAGE FOR FORM—THE ROAD NOT TAKEN

Uneasy about the epigrammatic brevity of Freud's "anatomy is destiny" and Wilde's "nature imitates art," let me add less pithily: anatomy is one of the arts; biology is less biological than poetry; rhythm, rhythm—the shudder at the spine—is destiny. Thomas Mann calls this destiny *"Leiden und Formtrieb* [suffering and form-drive]" in his definition of poetry. But *Formtrieb* may also be accompanied by happy fulfillment, not only by *Leiden*. What is insufferable about the cult of suffering is the unintended implication that genius is an infinite capacity for faking pains.

A more classical, less Teuton-romantic sense of form is conveyed by Paul Valéry's definition: "A man is a poet if his imagination is stimulated by disciplines." Contemporary avant-garde, once associated with antiform, reached full circle at the moment when Theodore Solotaroff, founder of a leading avant-garde magazine, *New American Review,* admitted in 1974: "New consciousness does not necessarily require new forms in literature. . . ." And it was, after all, not a reactionary but the greatest innovator of new consciousness, Charles Baudelaire, who wrote: "Je hais le mouvement qui déplace les lignes."

"To what tune," asked Thomas Hardy, "danceth this Immense?" To the tune you feel it through—most likely pentameter if you are American, English, German, or Russian; caesura'd hexameter if you are French or Polish. But instead of a subjective relativist babel of scansion for this immense dance of our tidal earth, there is one objective biological common denominator: iambics—this *formal* poetry—with which our body has been in tune all along without knowing it.

Poetry is iambic pentameter if it can be scanned as such by a good ear. In his strongest passages, Whitman, too, was "all along" writing iambic pentameter rather than free verse, provided we can get around the way he broke up his pentameter lines. Have we the right to break them up differently? In principle, no, but in practice, perhaps yes—in the sense of D. H. Lawrence's "never trust the artist, trust the tale."

Listen to Whitman's rhythms and not to his nonpentameter line breaks, especially as the latter were partially motivated by a desire to seem more antitraditional than he was.

The situation gets trickier with W. C. Williams, who urges "a basic attack upon the whole realm of structure in the poem." Would he, as a medical doctor, "basically attack" that strictly pounding body-structure which is the poem's structure as well? Just when meter and rhyme seem finished in post-Williams America, their rebirth is about to begin by pioneering deeper into our own bodily palimpsest.

The freshness, the innovativeness of form lie not behind but ahead. The two weaknesses of English rhymes (their paucity in an uninflected language and their consequent predictability) are combated not by abandoning rhyme but by extending it vigorously into new areas of metric and biological sensation. Consider, then, the advantages of rhyming the first one or two syllables of each line with the last syllables of another or the same line. In view of rhyme's chain-reaction effect upon rhythm, this conservation-through-reform would also combat the sloppy neglect of opening syllables and the pompous exaggeration of closing ones, thereby also replacing, in the two opening syllables, the slackness of underaccentuation with the excitement of the spondee as an expression of strong feeling. For instance this (unused) *Archer* fragment:

DIALOGUE WITH SELF:
THE NAZARENE PACINGS IN GETHSEMANE

I

Doubting in a garden:
When will I climb out?

Crying on a tree:
Me, father? Why?

2

Sleeping in a quarry
Three nights deep:
Lout or fool,
Who'll carve me out?

3

Doubting in a garden
Then?—And now.
Pacing till I fall?
—Always.

The opening spondee would end the isolation of the line-unit and reduce the slurp of diction by no longer allowing the reader to hurry through opening syllables as if they were deadwood. The spondee!— this binocular staccato of calm frenzy and slow suddenness: how, without a new formal fusing of rhyme and spondee, can poetry regain a Keatsian full-throatedness?

The aim of our invented form—christen it "crisscross"—is not to play some cerebral game but to deepen emotionally the counterresonances of ear and pulse; this is achieved by involving the entire line, and not just the last syllable, in rhyme's cumulative sonorities. These, in turn, will supply more threads to weave together a longer stanza, a broader, many-voiced vox humana. Rhyme staleness will be replaced by new rhymes never before found in literature; no rhyming dictionary or other mechanical prop lists the new sounds found in opening syllables. To avoid distracting from the new frontward shift of ear-attention, no final syllables may, in this form, rhyme with each other. But rhyme they must (though from now on with front-words) since the ear still requires, in final words, the dying fall of the second shoe. Countless popular, often jocular expressions like "golden oldie" suggest that first-syllable rhymes are not a synthetic concoction but in the grain of common speech.[5]

Later craftsmen will be devising better form-experiments in the 1990s. The imperative to observe throughout is that each strict new form must be the "inevitable" expression of an organic flowering and not the arbitrary fidget of a gymnast. In time this imperative will again

be forgotten; then a free verse revolt will again excruciate the forget-
ters. (This is a prediction that the new nonformalist form-movement
will last forty years.)

In *Archer in the Marrow*, the crisscross is sometimes on the same line
("All.gods.were.immortal.") and sometimes yokes a couplet:

> Image of ambush,
> Hushingly dim

Or, it gets internalized as throughout the opening *Up* cycle:

> Skull Hill was so scruffed a rug that the threads unmeshed;
> My reach fleshed out too late,—a leper's hug.

But form should be felt, not noticed, lest a means become an end;
hence the crisscross rhymes should more often be not a couplet, as
above, but several lines apart. This process can only be clarified by
concrete examples of actual practice, preferably from other, better poets.
Soon there may be such examples but, as yet, not one is at hand; so
Critical Inquiry diagramed an *Archer* excerpt (see page 227) as the only
way to visualize the farflung interweavings of the new form. Unlike
iambics and unlike rhymed couplets and quatrains, less central forms
do indeed get outworn, i.e., form gone bloodless into prettiness, gone
genteel into lacquer, or gone clarion call into uplift. Or else, form
gone maestro into the calisthenics of technique: dost thou think, because
thou art virtuoso, there shall be no more cakes and ale? Unhoned form
does tend to get just plain cluttered, what with cloying or jingly
rhymes and the pirouettes of coy villanelles. In such cases, free verse
(a Ginsbergian howl or the linguistic re-Americanization of Williams)
does indeed come as a liberation. A brief one. For it depends on readers
being both steeped in the old forms and dictions, and sick of them.
Whenever a new generation comes along, unsteeped in the old order,
the free verse loses its frisson of contrast and becomes outworn in turn.
A new form of form then liberates us from the liberator.

The way to avoid being numbed by inorganic metrics is to release
the drunken free play (but with a sober trained ear) of rhythm's coun-
terflux, its antimetronome undercurrents, and to release the fruitful
contradiction between visceral connotation and cerebral denotation.
This free play and this fruitfulness had been banalized away by the

"LIDS": CRISSCROSSINGS DIAGRAMED

Image of ambush,
Hushingly dim;
Gold-bellied hornet
Hanging from ceiling.
Torment is dangling
Feelers at man.
Antennae are trailing from
Gold chandelier;
Fearing no ambush,
Home come the children,
Bearing a dutiful
Image of sky
Holding a teddy bear,
Children are sleeping,
Famished by scrimmage,
Depressingly old.
Image of ambush,
Noise on the ceiling:
Hum that accuses
Hangs from the sky
Seeping caressingly,
Gold of the ambush
Oozes on sleepers
Beautiful poison,
Sky's ancient fangs.

time of the Georgians (exceptions were the spindrift grace notes of Walter de la Mare and the bitter riptide rhythms of Charlotte Mew). Banalization provoked not only the 1912 revolt (that is, the founding of *Poetry* magazine, Harriet Monroe, Amy Lowell, Harold Monro's American verse issue of *Poetry Review,* and the symbolic clash of the simultaneous 1912 publication of *Georgian Poetry* and Pound's *Ripostes*). Banalization also provoked the second triumph of free verse rebels after the formalist 1950s. The earlier reaction against outworn conformities was international and not just English-speaking. Or is it coincidence that 1912 also saw the publication of Anna Akhmatova's first book of poems, *Evening,* and the accompanying Russian Acmeist reaction (Mandelstam, Gumilev) against the mystic vagueness established internationally by French symbolism in poetry and by *art nouveau* in décor? But the greatness of Akhmatova and Mandelstam, in contrast with the shallower precisions of what Pound called Amygism, may be related to the older form-sense—plus the younger lyricism—of these martyred Russians.

Is modern poetry (post-1912) a tale told by an Eliot, full of Pound and fury, signifying Williams? These bull-slaying toreadors have now become *sacred cows.* Modernism (meaning image, not lilt; "conversational" line, not meter) is now the outdated Royal Academy it once rightly fought. Suppose the 1912 modernists had not been assured success by the generous enthusiasms of Pound, the papal infallibilities and glamourous anti-glamour of Eliot, and in later years the truly noble integrity of W. C. Williams (his *Paterson* a wonderful epic violating his own theories). There would have been major losses (we are all grandchildren of Harriet Monroe). But only losses? Is it a gain that a traditionalist of prosody like Millay, now neglected, is less read than, say, Bukowski?

The road-not-taken would have led—can still lead—not through Eliot's conventional Victorian-Georgian foes but through the unconventional delicate rhymes of de la Mare, the vigorous ones of Hardy, the agonized iambic pentameters of Charlotte Mew, and the ecstatic ones of Hart Crane and Roethke, with Frost (not the folksy fake but the fierce fox) central rather than peripheral.

Suppose Yeats's road had lasted long enough to establish as a norm the flexible extra-beat tetrameters of *Purgatory,* attained only on his deathbed. His earlier tetrameters were too monotonously caesura'd or else too ballad-style bumpy, the two factors that, in general, still sabotage four-beat lines. But his quick half-suppressed extra beats, such as scanning "being" as one syllable, kept the accent straining excitingly against the meter instead of numbingly with it. The *Purgatory* tetrameters, plus the magic subsurface trimeters of his pentameter blank verse, would have reformed our language's traditional meters from within and thereby made unnecessary the free-verse revolution from without. Better a reformist Turgot than a 1789, which then merely becomes a new kind of Bourbon academy. This road-not-taken would have preserved what today's poetry often lacks, a good ear.

Even the revivers of metrical strictness today are leery of rhyme as "lacking surprise." Yet functional rhyme never ceases to startle by the unstrict regularity and the strict variations of its interweavings. This is why a Petrarchan sonnet offers more possibilities (unless one is Shakespeare) than a Shakespearean sonnet. Rhyme's worst vice is not being boring but being lurid, as when the rhymes of Poe's "Ulalume" writhe so contortedly that you can't tell whether this spaghetti of cobras is wrestling, murdering, or copulating. Meanwhile there will always be the imperfect "perfection" of the formalists—a charming minor genre, not felt in the heart—whose rhyme and meter are so smooth that they cry out, like pomaded hair, to be mussed up.

Is rhyme tyrant or liberator? In *Swann's Way,* Proust defines "great poets" as those whom "the tyranny of rhyme forces into the discovery of their finest lines." A Nietzsche letter of February 22, 1884, shows how the dance of form can be a liberating kind of tyranny: "My style is a dance, a play of all kinds of symmetries and a mocking leap over these symmetries. This holds true even in the choice of vowels."

It was noted earlier that in practice Williams felicitously violated his own theories. The bane of modern American poetry is the fact that so many free-verse poets are following his theories, not his practice. Williams was, of course, not writing formless verse but strict American-voice rhythms, for which his ear was the best ever. To understand his structurings, you must read his poems as if each line ended with a period or comma, something they rarely do. If you read the lines as enjambed, they too often sound like prose. Here he unintentionally resembles Pope, the strictest of formalists, whose lines are also rarely enjambed. So the reader's body responds to two kinds of duo-level tension in Williams: the eye's run-over line straining against the ear's end-stop line, and the formal English straining against the colloquial Yank. Some readers, however, will detect a subterranean third; the oldfashioned, conventional meters that had dulled his first book, he later hurled to Hades with such excessive self-disgust that they bounced back in from below, despite himself.

These rhythm-conflicts trigger his true genius: it is not enough to celebrate only his just-folks talk of icebox plums and red wheelbarrows. Far from being either American or divinely simple, such diction and imagery are the sophisticated strategy of *le faux naïf*—very foreign and very French.

Much modernism isn't modern, being a veneered version of the Victorianism it attacks. Thus Cummings is a nineteenth-century love-slob beneath the pseudo-tough disguise of tricky typography. And the "Mauberley" Pound is a disguised pre-Raphaelite, often a better one than the pre-Raphaelites; even the "Greek" paganism of the Cantos is more Swinburne than Greece.

Doctors disagree. W. C. Williams, a doctor as well as a great poet, said: "The attack must concentrate on the rigidity of the poetic foot." Galen, another doctor, A.D. 130–200, wrote that not only our feet (Greek meaning of iambs) but our heartbeats are rigidly iambic—with death the alternative. What joins footsteps and heartbeats are lungs. In his "Conversation About Dante," Ossip Mandelstam writes: "The metrical foot is the inhalation and exhalation of the step. . . . The step, linked with breathing and saturated with thought, Dante understood as the beginning of prosody." If the inhale and exhale of the lungs takes five times as long as a slightly rapid systole-diastole of the heart, may we, then, redefine iambic pentameter as one breathful of excited hearts?

You can't heave out iambic pentameter (Pound, Canto LXXX: "To break the pentameter, that was the first heave") without amputating foot and heart. In your own body, a comparable heave could cost you your life: "In cardiopulmonary resuscitation, the new technique for keeping alive victims of 'sudden death' is by mouth-to-mouth breathing and rhythmical pressure on the chest," writes John Nims. "One breath is given for every five of the chest compressions which are substitute heartbeats." How Shakespearean of nature! It is not artificial but *natural* that most poetry in our language has been iambic pentameter. When a poet protested to me wrathfully, "The iamb's not a normal measure of speech," I invited him to scan his protest.

Ours is indeed "the age of Pound" (apt phrase by one of our subtlest and most original critics, the "Poundian" Hugh Kenner). And many are the blessings Pound brought us, ranging from the rediscovery of poets from China and Provence to the rediscovery of enthusiasm—and producing a re-sensitized poetry "as well written as prose." But is it philistine to ask whether the blessings are mixed? Pound's most attractive aspects, such as his gallant championing of loners, get lost in his epigone admirers. Unlike Kenner, most Poundians have made a rigid new conformity of this nonconformist. Pound wisely foresaw this in an only recently published letter of 1920: "Any damn thing I put down is susceptible of being made into a new academicism."

* * *

At least one aspect of metaphor—and indeed of all other links between separate images and thoughts in poetry—overlaps with at least one major function of rhyme. By linking two words of similar sound and of either similar or opposite meanings, rhyme can link these images or thoughts in two ways: reassurance and surprise. To link similarities is reassuring (often tediously so, as with "love" and "dove"). To link opposites—into a new bifocal vision—is a surprise. (When mere half-resemblances or half-differences are linked, then rhyme blurs over, becoming a nonfunctional frill.) More interestingly, rhyme links the opposites not just of image but of lilt talk. Rhyme is (like Keats' name) writ in water; it is the canal of scansions; it connects those competing torrents and undertows that make certain marvelous unscannable whirlpools in Beddoes, Hardy and Heaney. Without rhyme, no concord of discord.

Increasingly rhyme came to be chosen not for these linking functions but for useless ornamentation or pedantry. At this point, free verse became an indispensable garbage disposal unit. But the junking of rhyme altogether results in an insufferable disproportion: the sacrifice of ear to eye, of pulsebeat to the voyeurism of tropes. If Blake saw through, and not with, the eye, then the eye-obsessed poet of today must learn again to "see" through the ear (which in turn—as in Marlowe and Hart Crane—"hears" through the eye).

Have the would-be conservatives conserved any better than the free verse avant-garde of yesteryear? Before radical chic, came a now-forgotten antiradical chic. In 1950, when Alexandrianizing critics were dragging the muse from the sublime to the meticulous, poetry was being left to the English departments, despite Clemenceau's warning against leaving war to the generals. The consequence was the anti-academic overreaction of the "howling" open-roaders. Perhaps we acted mistakenly, we of the lyricizing third camp who blamed the academic hermeticism too exclusively on the New Critics, who were, after all, considerable poets and in most things our betters. The real mischief of the 1950s came from the *nouveaux* New Critics, the sacred calves of the graduate schools. Trained seals of jargon (to vary the metaphor), how nimbly they swallowed some fishy explication de texte in midair, leaping through hoop after hoop of the criticism of the criticizing of criticism. These epigones and their beat and hip enemies were, of course, opposite sides of the same coin: form made sterile or form uprooted.

Just as rooted lawful liberty is equally betrayed by reactionary authoritarianism and by its consequence, radical anarchy, so aesthetic form is equally betrayed by the anarchic formlessness of the barbaric yawpers and by the dead formalism of the elegant wincers. Formalism, by being an -ism, kills form by hugging it to death, whereas form-lessness kills it openly. Poetry's return to living form in the 1990s will supersede both extremes. Maxim: no to formless wildness; no to the rigorous strictness of rigor mortis; yes to strict wildness. Only so can content and form embrace in equal pride.

Only a death-hug formalist would use the fatuous phrase "perfect form" or would rewrite *"l'art pour l'art"* as form for its own sake. Poetry is better left undefined (only Procrustes would generalize uniqueness); but if a definition be demanded at pistolpoint, then let us define it as expressive form. That is, form for the sake of expressing an imperfection known as humanity. And ornery humanity will never be the abstract perfection of the world; it will continue to be, if we may pontificate more papally than Pope, the world's "riddle, jest, and wonder."

Not all defenses of form are here being endorsed nor all free verse excommunicated. For example, Robert Frost's overquoted tennis net justification of form is actually an unfair kind of challenge to free verse because it is inorganic. Unlike the throb of lung or groin, a net is not part of our living protoplasm. Furthermore, the net metaphor fails to evoke the tension between form and content and the tension between simultaneous rival rhythms of form. A poem is not an either-or situation between form and content or between two rival rhythms. Nor is it a calculated compromise (50–50 or 80–20) between such alternatives. The achieved poem is both alternatives fully and both at the same instant. To be 100 percent form yet 100 percent content is an unmathematical miracle: its parts are greater than the sum of its wholes. Meanwhile the sterile formalists discredit form by playing the net without the tennis.

During an authentic, not just modish tremor of poetry, what precisely is happening to poet and reader? The answer can involve either mechanistic or humanistic science, i.e., the quantitative research of a Kinsey Report or the broader humanity of the early, not yet paranoid Wilhelm Reich. The former is reductive—will too much someday be made of our valid contention that poetry, like love, has an indispensable physical base? Will there, accordingly, be analysts quantifying (when they should be qualifying as well) poetry's rhythm-correlation with body waves or even with alpha brain waves? The very thought of such measurers is grotesque enough to inspire us to a Perelman-style skit, in which Masters and Johnson, both played by Groucho Marx, strap down a protesting Sophocles.

But such farce will be avoided if science shows an uncharacteristic, but not impossible, modesty in the presence of art's unmeasurability. The analyst's vaunted "third ear" will have to listen not only to all relevant chemical-muscular-arterial responses but also to humanity's value codes of beauty, including ethical and religious values as well as aesthetic ones; nothing narrower does justice to the full gamut of imagination and aspiration. What else can give to airy beauty a local habitation and a name but that joint mind-body rhythm which makes lyric communication so uniquely intense?

Facing mental and physical extremes, the prisoners of Nazi death camps would often express in poetry their gropings for a sustaining moral order: in such demanding structures as sonnet and terza rima[6]; and this while interrupted by torture and terror. Here form expresses an ultimate assertion of humanity.

3. PURE FORM?—THE POUND CONTROVERSY REVISITED

Mention of death-camp poets raises a question: can form flourish in a moral vacuum? Logically, yes; psychologically, no. In practice, how can our psyche avoid a partial overlap between ethics and aesthetics? The mix-up of both is what makes us human. Form is there for concentrating our feelings, not for propaganda. But our feelings include not only our private relationships but our private response to public evil. You may loftily choose not to respond to mass murder and to anti-Black and anti-Jewish racism, but your nonresponse is a response nonetheless. Sometimes being "above the battle" is a way of being part of the battle on evil's side.

Here is a brief memoir of the 1950s. This fragment of autobiography is presented in the hope that the first-person-singular of yesterday can become of general interest to the "you" of today by throwing light on two ongoing critical issues: pure form in poetry and free debate about form. Both these issues came to a head in 1949 when a distinguished literary jury, at the Library of Congress, awarded Pound's *Pisan Cantos* the Bollingen prize, then America's highest literary honor. My essay of April 1950 in *Commentary* magazine disagreed with the judges; it also went out of its way to honor their motives. The judges were being loyal to modernist poetry (ambiance of Pound, Eliot, the New Critics); they were not being pro-fascist, as charged by Robert Hillyer in *Saturday Review*. Such charges were not taken seriously by those who "counted" in literature and only served to make it look as if the persecuted martyr were Pound himself rather than the millions tortured to death by fascism. Actually Pound had just been rescued, on grounds of "insanity," from a treason trial; other Axis broadcasters, like "Lord Haw Haw," had just been sentenced to death. According to E. F. Torrey's *Roots of Treason,* 1983, Pound was saved as "insane" by doctors lying under pressure.

This revisiting of the controversy is mainly literary. As for the politicos: Italian neo-fascists gained status by misusing the "official" (Library of Congress) nature of the award, while anti-fascist American Congressmen repudiated such Government sponsorship. Both groups were misconstruing the award as political. But both political furors were short-lived, abandoning the controversy to the literary community, where the non-fascist (pure art) kind of Poundians had almost every prestige-exuding name on their side.

Though the aesthetic defenders of Pound's *Pisan Cantos* were *l'art pour l'art,* he himself intended them as *l'art pour la politique.* Far from being "obscure" (as alleged by his more philistine detractors), the book's main message is clear: to mourn the fall of Troy, "the Troy of the Axis powers,"[7] and to compare to the unheeded warnings of Cassandra his own Radio Rome warnings against "Jewish" Roosevelt's "Jew-Nited States." Dwight Macdonald told me that Pound was "irate" at Macdonald's defending the Bollingen award as nonpolitical and purely literary; it was for its message that Pound wanted the book judged.

Hillyer's crude *Saturday Review* attack was an easy-to-refute minor distraction, overemphasized by the Pound-Eliot establishment as if it were mainstream and then triumphantly refuted. By attacking not just Pound but twentieth-century poetry as a whole, Hillyer played into the hands of those who wanted to identify the cause of the *Pisan Cantos* with that of poetry itself. By counterattacking the *Saturday Review* silliness with self-righteous big-name petitions (a loyalty oath poets were pressed to sign), the award's defenders had a pretext for ignoring the more serious, less easily refuted attacks on the award, such as mine in *Commentary*.

Modernism and "pure" form—not the same but in 1949–50 allied— deserve to be debated on their merits, not *ad hominem*. One might have expected such a level of "Southern gentlefolk" civility from the New Critic school, then dominating key English departments, as it was a school priding itself on omitting biographic influences. But the reaction concentrated less on the issue than on the writer who raised it—and not only on my wicked motives but on and against my uninvolved lyrics. It was as if potential dissenters were being given an object lesson.

The lesson had its effect. Among influential critics, only Robert Gorham Davis and Irving Howe wrote public expressions of agreement. One influential editor, while privately agreeing, said I must stop criticizing what he called "the Pound-Eliot-Tate establishment," or I would "no longer be publishable." Was something not wrong with existing standards when one's poems were no longer judged on their merits or demerits?

Many others, such as John Berryman, reacted even more violently. Evidently disloyalty did not include someone who broadcasted for the enemy in wartime—that was considered "nonconformism." Instead, disloyalty became defined as someone who disagreed with the literary hierarchs.

The Pound-Eliot modernist achievement gave its unachieving epigones their grad-school power base, but this explains only superficially their particular identification with Pound. It doesn't explain, for example, the downright frenzied identification felt by so major an achiever as the honest and independent Robert Lowell. The profounder explanation is that he and most poets, understandably feeling persecuted by society, identified compulsively with two images: the poet behind barbed wire (Pound interned at Pisa when Hitler lost) and the poet in the madhouse. While, of course, defending Pound against censors, chauvinists, and the middlebrow kind of anti-modernism, still I could not help thinking of the six million souls who expired in a somewhat different cage.

Unlike the right and left totalitarians, we should never judge art by its politics. But this was not a matter of politics or economics; it was a matter of ethics, a metaphysics of evil. Evil does indeed fall into the purview of aesthetic criticism because it parches empathy and hence the artist's creative imagination. Lacking empathy, the artist lacks Keats's "negative capability," a prerequisite for art. To summarize my 1950 argument in one sentence: when Ezra Pound was joking about genocide ("fresh meat on the Russian steppes," the most callous joke about mass murder ever penned by a poet), Pound's humanity narrowed, his art shrank.

Similarly he was impoverishing his empathy (and hence his creativity) by his radio appeals to our soldiers in Italy against "President Rosenfeld" and "the kikery of the Jew-Nited States." Orwell's comment (*Partisan Review,* May 1949) used the word "evil," not "politics":

> I saw it stated in an American periodical that Pound only broadcast on the Rome radio when "the balance of his mind was upset." . . . This is plain falsehood. Pound was an ardent follower of Mussolini as far back as the 1920s. . . . His broadcasts were disgusting. I remember at least one in which he approved the massacre of the East European Jews and "warned" the American Jews that their turn was coming. . . . He *may* be a good writer (I must admit that I personally have always regarded him as an entirely spurious writer), but the opinions he has tried to disseminate in his works are evil.

Before he died, Pound said he regretted anti-Semitism. On what grounds? Empathy at last? No, on grounds of its being what he called "a suburban prejudice." Those tortured six million turned out to be a casualty of manners, not evil. Auschwitz got soundly snubbed as an underbred suburb. Ah, if only Hitler had been urbane . . .

Recently I have again been debating these issues on campus speaking tours. The most frequent rebuttal by a new generation of pro-Pound liberals is to compare the Cantos to *The Merchant of Venice*. Did not that play express the deplorable anti-Semitism of Shakespeare's society yet transcend it by poetic genius? So was Pound not—by sheer genius—transcending the anti-Semitism of his chosen fascist society? Not quite; context is all. Shakespeare's play was not part of a genocidal holocaust, did not deprive Shylock of humanity, and did not impoverish his art by lack of feeling for his adversary. There is a world of difference—as ethics and as pure aesthetic form—between Pound's "fresh meat" and Shakespeare giving Shylock the common humanity of "I am a Jew. If you prick us, do we not bleed?"

Considered as pure sound, pure form, not content, are lines like the following beautiful poetry? They are quoted at random from the *Pisan Cantos:* "The goyim go to saleable slaughter" for "the yidd . . . David Rex the prime s.o.b. . . . Petain defended Verdun while Blum was defending a bidet." My critique also quoted with admiration the lovely lines in the same book, including the poignant "pull down thy vanity" passage. Which lines outweigh which? Rightly or wrongly, the well-intentioned Bollingen judges set a momentous precedent—the split between form and ethics—for American letters ever after.

* * *

It was a philosophic mistake to see the holocaust or gulag as politics rather than evil; this contributed to a literary mistake: the revival of propaganda poetry. Most rhymed editorializing works neither as poetry nor as propaganda. This unoriginal conclusion does not justify an ivory-tower condescension toward politics. Politics (above all, the bread-and-butter politics of economics) is worth whatever energy its partisans muster; more power to them. And may that energy be mustered on the side of fallible yet self-surpassing humanity; not on the side of inhuman abstractions, bloodily inflicted on human beings for their own good. It is important to protect art from meddling politicians. Important but not sufficient. Likewise art, though it can meddle where it pleases if it meddles beautifully, must never prostitute itself to ugly political rhetoric.

To sum up our revisiting: what may be needed in the 1990s is an impure human-scale form that is broad enough for ethical empathy but not for reductive propagandizing.

4. 1987 POSTSCRIPT

In an essay relating biology to aesthetic form, an unavoidable subtopic is: how does old age alter not only content but rhythm and technique? This impact on technique has never been probed, aesthetically or physiologically. What's really going on in the marrow of art as well as of body? The artist can't help but bark livelier while still in Dylan Thomas's young-dog days. As the aging perceptions lose broadness, they dig for depth. The blind sharpen their hearing, the deaf their sight. And they cling to ungrandiose poignant nuances to replace their lost grand piano.

Age often brings absurdities of contents (the old-sage stance masking old Polonius, the Wordsworth debacle). But age often also brings triumphs of form, new undertones and nuances. These triumphs may result from defeats, the creaking limbs of old age. For the creaking limbs have their stylistic correlative in harsher rhythms and more austere tones, challengingly abrupt. It is triumph *and* defeat when the older poet despises—as shallow—his earlier, smoother melodies. He gets numbed by the rhyming of syllables accented too obviously (electro-shocked once too often, the frog leg won't respond). He turns to a fresher music, such as a rhyming of unaccented last syllables, thereby accenting them "against their will," wrenching a trochee into an iamb. Here, in conclusion, is a frivolous try at illustrating each of these creaky form-changes.

PORTRAIT OF THE ARTIST AS AN OLD DOG[8]

I.
Fat grins, fat blurbs, fat stances: all gets honed.
Old poets are high-cheekboned.

Wildly mild, serenely fierce,
Old poets have green ears.

Too proud to sponge, they won't even ask you the time.
Brother, can you spare a dime?

When they play Elder Statesman, they're way out of tune,
    But they've perfect pitch in their funnybone.

New tricks you can't teach them, but their "outdated forms"
    Shall be your grandchild's norms.

They embarrass both Wellfleet and Osh Kosh by not keeping
    Standard Time.
    Hypocrite lecteur—my clone—can you spare a rhyme?

II.

What is fit torture for pelts that let you peep
Deep?

Young poets' hugs enfold
Mirrors. Old

Poets *are* mirrors . . . showing you not
Your face, but—?

Bone-covered monsters are hard to rout;
Old poets are turtles—they're inside-out.

They're so like you that they're from . . . Mars.
So unlike that their marrow's yours.

Pelt splits—marrow swells—to slough
Six decades' fluff.

Marrow crams so innermost a shelf
It's furtive even toward itself.

Not so the face; its tic
Is public.

Old po—flay them quick, they show
Marrow.

Notes

UP CYCLE

1. *Second death:* "Forgive us," said Pope John XXIII of the Final Solution's six million deaths, "for crucifying Thee a *second* time in their flesh."

2. *Chimney's Baal-bellied belch:* Referring to the smoke of burning corpses in Nazi death camps. See *Baal* in glossary.

HACKED CYCLE

1. *Leopards:* Greek illustrations of Dionysus-Bacchus show him riding in a cart pulled by leopards.

2. *East:* When used with a small "e" the sense is geographical; when used with a capital "E" it is religious, referring to the Christian motto "ex oriente lux" (out of the East, light).

3. *I'm flow:* Echo of the Greek philosopher Heraclitus: "All is flow."

4. *Fish:* Here lungfish becomes the archetype for man's self-surpassing defiance of sky, being our first air-breathing, land-invading ancestor.

5. *Comet-mane:* The word "comet" comes from the Greek word for long-haired (star).

ROUND CYCLE

1. *Asian war:* Here an analogy is being made between America's Vietnam and ancient Rome's bogging down in Asian Parthia.

2. *Burglar Caesar:* Here a Roman analogy with an American president's involvement in the Watergate burglary.

3. *Boat people:* Homeless refugees from Communist Vietnam, here seen as Joseph and Mary, looking for shelter with their child Jesus.

4. *1984 (other earth):* In the alternative universe, Orwell's nightmare world is treated as if it actually took place.

5. *Infinite love attained by infinite terror:* See *Jan Bockelsen* in glossary.

Note on Stage Version of "Round": When "Round" is read or staged apart from the book as a self-sufficient playlet, the preferred title is "Welcome to Tarsus." When it was staged in 1980 by the Lab Theater (Catholic University) of Washington, D.C., two speakers were used instead of one. The second actor stood for the first one's mirror image, spoke whatever stage directions could not be conveyed by gesture, and spoke the final section 9, at this point exchanging places in the mirror frame with the first actor. The Lab Theater did not end with section 9 but with a repetition—after 9—of section 1 and of the first six spoken lines of section 2. The Lab Theater also used movie screen projections to imitate Tarsus and Los Angeles and, in section 5, for Columbus falling off the edge of the world, Saint Lucrezia Borgia, etc. Each new section number requires lighting changes to alert the audience that a reversal is ahead: of speaker's disguise or of parallel earths.

TRANSITIONS

1. *All word-jugglers; even my black-sheep brother in Galilee/Punned forth a church on a rock:* Referring to Christ's pun on the name Peter; see *Peter* in glossary.

2. *Panic:* In its Greek origin meaning: Passers-by fell into a "panic" when faced by the god, Pan, at noon.

3. *Heathen Easters:* The Greek god Dionysus-Bacchus and the parallel Egyptian god Osiris were both annually hacked into scattered pieces, and reborn each spring, a pre-Christian (heathen) Easter.

WALTZ CYCLE

1. *A narrow fellow programmed me / With gene tapes, Xerox at the bone:* In her snake poem #986 beginning, "A narrow Fellow in the Grass," Emily Dickinson ends by feeling "And Zero at the Bone." Here "Zero" is deliberately misquoted as "Xerox" in view of the "apple" offered by the snake in Eden, here the Apple computer of modern technology.

2. *The woman thou gavest me:* Adam's reference to Eve in the Old Testament.

BREAD CYCLE

1. *Green Mass:* Coined as Dionysian pagan alternative to the black and white moralizing (or immoralizing) of Christian white mass (or satanic black mass). In the opening of the Gods Cycle, Green Mass is sharply differentiated from the "green-gone-formless" of such 1960s' counterculture books as Charles Reich's *The Greening of America.*

2. *Cities of the Calf and of the Plain:* Here representing monetary greed (Golden Calf) and sexual greed (the plain of Sodom and Gomorrah).

3. *College widow:* The local college-town belle, gradually aging, here making a virtue of necessity by becoming a nun.

4. *Our milt does more than Miltown can / To justify man's ways to man:* Deliberately misquoting from A. E. Housman's observation that "malt does more than Milton can / to justify God's ways to man."

5. *The wound and the bow:* This title of Edmund Wilson's most famous book refers to the wound of the Greek archer Philoctetes and the psychological overcompensation for wounds.

ROGUE CYCLE

1. *That Nature does betray the hearts that love her:* Misquoting William Wordsworth's lines from "Tintern Abbey": "My dear, dear Sister! And this prayer I make / Knowing that Nature never did betray / The heart that loved her."

2. *I 'is' a Nother:* Derived from a line by Rimbaud in his letter of May 13, 1871: "Je est un autre" (I is another [someone else]).

SALT CYCLE

1. *Tears, idle tears:* Quoted from Tennyson, here in connection with the ocean's salt bath of a mollusc's first "eyes."

2. *But hero's trio, blood-sweat-tears:* Echo of Churchill's speech of resistance during the Battle of Britain in World War II.

3. *Sacre du bed-Spring:* Coined to combine Stravinsky's "Rites of Spring" ballet with the erotic bounce of bedsprings.

4. *Amniotic Sea:* From "Amnion" (Greek diminutive of *amnos*, lamb): membrane of sac enclosing embryo: filled with saline fluid replicating ocean environment on land.

5. *Urine brine:* "Normally the fetus voids urine into the surrounding amniotic brine fluid about once an hour."—*New York Times,* May 26, 1981.

6. *Patronize your local gallows-tree:* Allusion to the hanged man giving

the ocean back his various landlocked saline fluids from his various apertures, the last one being—at snap of spine—his semen.

7. *Small death:* Orgasm (from the French "petite mort").

8. *Mandrake-shrieks:* From the white seed of a hanged man, according to folklore, sprouts a magic mannikin or man-shaped root, called "mandrake" or "alraune," that shrieks when uprooted.

9. *Romantic Agony:* Title of book about romanticism-gone-morbid by Mario Praz.

STAIN CYCLE

1. *'Hanging men and women for the wearing of the green':* This line from a patriotic Irish ballad is here used in a very different sense of green; see *green mass* as defined in Note 1 under Bread Cycle.

2. *More Wings than Wings Can Bear:* If on stage, these feminine endings of unmatching consonants should get spoken staccato so as to bring out the falsity of the rhymes, paralleling the falsifying (concept-imposing) modern eye. Hypothesis: the direct vision of cave art in Dordogne, each deer unique, became generalized away after the invention of language. See Down Cycle.

3. *Caps of bells under bays:* "Bays" refers to a crown for bards in old Greece, and "Caps of bells" refers to the jingly mock-crown of court jesters.

4. *Trampoline spider:* Denoting the heart bouncing on its web of veins.

PISH CYCLE

1. *'Tis pity she's a bore':* Variation of the title of John Ford's play, *'Tis Pity She's a Whore.*

2. *Else a great bug in prison lies:* Variation on John Donne's line from "The Ecstasy": "Else a great Prince in prison lies."

EYES CYCLE

1. *Urb and orb:* From the Papal invocation, "urbem et orbem": addressing the city (Rome) and the globe.

2. *'I'll see my Pilot face to face':* Reference to God taken from Tennyson's poem, "Crossing the Bar."

3. *If hooks prick us, don't we bleed?:* Reference to Shakespeare's Shylock when he says: "I am a Jew. If you prick us, do we not bleed?"

4. *Assyrian beards:* The long oiled beards of the murderous kings of ancient war-like Assyria.

5. *Penny 'for your thoughts':* Here the penny represents the coins a mortician puts down on cadaver eyes to keep their lids from popping open.

BOOK CYCLE

1. *The beast-with-poor-posture:* Irreverent reference to Yeats' overquoted "And what rough beast . . . slouches towards Bethlehem to be born."

2. *"When Pan paid his obol to Charon":* The moment Christ was born, according to ancient legend, a wail arose from the hills and waters: "Great Pan is dead!" The obol coin was Charon's fee for ferrying the dead to Hades.

3. *Thou hast conquered, O tanned Californian:* Here used to reverse Algernon Charles Swinburne's line about Christ: "thou hast conquered, O pale Galilean." See *Julian the Apostate* in glossary.

4. *'Nicene two-as-one':* Referring to Christianity's official Nicene creed of the year 325 that proclaimed God and Christ to be a single deity.

5. *Wrong hill:* Olympus.

AUSCHWITZ CYCLE

1. *The Birth of Travesty from the Spirit of Bayreuth:* Here a deliberate misquoting (with reference to Wagner's Bayreuth shrine) of Nietzsche's early, but later partly repudiated, defense of Wagner, entitled "The Birth of Tragedy from the Spirit of Music."

2. *Caligari Calvary: The Cabinet of Dr. Caligari* was a surrealist German movie of the 1920s, where all lines, being filtered through mad eyes, were askew. Here Hitler's Wagnerian extermination program is called "a Caligari Calvary."

3. Throughout this prose paragraph, all statements in *single* quotes are quoted verbatim from Nietzsche's writings of the 1880s. His predictions of the "slaughter of Jews" by a Wagnerian "Volk Reich" were almost entirely overlooked amid the gibberish of his madness (see especially his letter of January 6, 1889). A documented source for several of these quotes of madness comes from Podach, *Nietzsche's Zusammenbruch* (Nietzsche's Breakdown).

4. *Lib-eq-frat:* Abbreviation for "liberty-equality-fraternity"—motto of French Revolution, 1789.

5. *The Kali Banality of Evil:* An amalgam of the Shakespearean monster Caliban, the Hindu death god Kali, and Hannah Arendt's much-quoted phrase about Nazis, "the banality of evil."

6. *'Rather clown than be Saintly'* and *'should have stuck to his verses':* These two *single*-quote citations from the preceding four lines of the text are free

translations from Nietzsche's *Ecce Homo,* 1889, IV, I ("Ich will kein Heiliger sein, lieber noch ein Hanswurst") and from the third edition of his *Birth of Tragedy from the Spirit of Music,* "Attempt at Self-Criticism," 1886 (italics in original): "Sie hätte *singen* sollen, diese 'neue Seele'—und nicht reden."

7. *Lampshade:* Referring to the use of human skin for lampshades in Nazi death camps.

PROLOGUE TO PART THREE

1. *Of all your drained cosmos: like Boaz, must cold-foot Entropy press / A hot-water bottle named Ruth:* Here Eve's indignant reference to the figure of Ruth in Old Testament, where her young body warmed old Boaz. (See *Book of Ruth,* 3:7, 14: "And she came softly, and uncovered his feet, and laid her down. . . . And she lay at his feet until the morning.") Here Ruth represents womanhood as a force of warm humanity in a cold mechanical world.

2. *What does woman want:* Freud's famous unanswered query, here answered by Eve voice.

3. *Moon-wound's witch broth:* Monthly (i.e., moon-coordinated) bleeding.

MEK CYCLE

1. *The beep's in the meadow, the borsht's in the corn:* "Beep" refers to a Geiger counter warning of dangerous atomic radiation. Borsht, being the best-known Russian soup, is symbolic of the Soviet impact on corny America.

2. *When the wind blows you, the tuna will glow:* After the American atomic tests in the Pacific, Japanese fishermen reported an odd glow in their tuna catch, hundreds of miles to the east.

3. The *Terra's Manifesto* refers to the familiar Terence quote of "humani nihil a me alienum puto" (cf. glossary); the *Mek Manifesto* placard, dated 1895, was the prophetic manifesto of an American engineer.

4. *Gothic:* The "dark ages" aspect of medieval life.

5. *Snow Against Rain:* Here, and throughout, snow and frost are shorthand for seasonal death, Pluto, entropy. In contrast, rain and green are equated with fertility, warmth, earth.

CORE CYCLE

1. *The Insulted and the Injured:* Title of Dostoyevsky's novel; here referring to the scorned potato.

2. *Tar:* To preserve the hanged criminal (as object lesson) from the inclemency of the elements, he was traditionally painted with a protective covering of black tar.

3. *Sweet Geiger sirens:* "Geiger" means "violinist" in German as well as the clicks that count atomic "radiance"; "sirens" means singers that lure as well as signals that warn.

TOWARD CYCLE

1. *'Mother, I cannot mind my wheel':* Classic fragment from Sappho as elaborated by Walter Savage Landor.

2. *'The lost traveller's* [sic—Blake's spelling] *dream under the hill':* Blake's evocative line.

3. *"Brightness falls from the air / Queens have died young and fair":* Thomas Nashe's evocative lines from "A Litany in Time of Plague."

4. *Blue flowers of romance:* Term borrowed from Novalis's (Friedrich von Hardenberg) ethereal symbolic phrase "die blaue Blume der Romantik"; here juxtaposed with "blue movies."

5. *A Sermon not on the Mount but on the mons:* Refers to mons Veneris, the female anatomy mount of Venus, in father's porn movie.

6. *Snuff:* Slang for porno movie where actors are actually killed.

7. *Edward, Edward:* Title and refrain of one of the most bloody-handed Scottish ballads, here identified with stone-wielding "Kid Cain" and the beastly depths to which man sinks when he tries to rise too soulfully high, hence last line and key rhyme motif of Toward Cycle.

THREADS CYCLE

1. *Badge:* Jews in Nazi Germany were forced to wear yellow stars.

2. *Vinegar. Zyklon-B / One pilgrim staff hasn't reblossomed:* Jews of Auschwitz ended up waiting—like Christ on his hill—for water. The "vinegar" they got instead was Zyklon-B poison gas, pouring into "stainless" hygienic shower rooms. Re "pilgrim staff": Tannhäuser was denied absolution for underground Venusberg till his deadwood staff bloomed again.

DOWN CYCLE

1. *Goat:* Animal associated with Dionysus, Pan, and the Eros instinct. Even today, Dionysus is being worshipped as a goat on the Greek island of Skyros.

2. *Midsea:* Coined word for the human centrality of the classical Mediterranean culture.

3. *Palms:* Palm leaves were strewn in front of Christ when he entered Jerusalem.

GODS CYCLE

1. *Nine egos deep:* The original ancient Homeric city of Troy was supposedly buried nine cities deep.

2. *The Fig cloacal and the Fountain chemic:* Here used by Aphrodite for the gender distinctions.

3. *Olives:* Here used as shorthand for the pagan Mediterranean and Aegean cultures.

EPILOGUE

1. *I am that I am:* From Old Testament, Exodus 3:14. This autobiographical announcement by God has been variously interpreted. Most scholars think it means: "I will be what I will be"—implying, according to Northrop Frye, "a process accomplishing itself," hence here the last line of a book and the first line of a new spiral.

APPENDIX

1. How much of Shakespeare's magic lies in his simultaneous use of Elizabethan five-beats and medieval four-beats in *Cymbeline* and even earlier? This much is known: Shakespeare read John Gower for his *Pericles* of 1608. Similarly, according to such researchers as Frank Brownlow, Shakespeare was probably steeped in Lydgate's irregular four-beat rhythms or "tumble beat." Such rough medieval octosyllabics underlie many iambic pentameters of Shakespeare's later plays; the resultant tremolo helps account for their unconscious appeal to readers bored by straight pentameter vibrations. Long before the celebrated Hopkins letter about "counterpoint," two-layer rhythms were at the core of our heritage—and, consequently, created two-layer emotional connotations.

Steeping oneself in the centuries of our language, one gets the impression that tetrameter was the original pattern of English metrics. Language never stands still; starting perhaps with the age of vowel shifts and certainly by the time of Elizabethan blank verse, pentameter became the most "natural" form, whether by custom or because it was biologically inherent. But tetrameter did not die within the supervening five beats. It went, so to speak, underground, making metrical guerrilla raids from below—sabotaging the fifth of the five reigning accents—whenever the line had to express conflicting emotions simultaneously.

The most interesting metric experiment of the last half century may be Yeats's play "Purgatory." There (driving pentameter below) tetrameter surfaced again. But with Yeats it was no longer the crude old ballad-style tetrameter, too patly caesura'd; it was now enriched both by quick unaccented syllables and slow spondees and was unrhymed and colloquial. Yeats died shortly after his "Purgatory" experiment, cutting short the creation of a more flexible, more nervously dramatic kind of blank verse.

2. This two-way scansion, our in-and-out of heart-lung-Eros as "spilt iambics," is developed at greater length in the Dionysian "Planted Poet" credo ending cycle nine, the Stain Cycle.

3. Despite Rimbaud's much-quoted "A noir, E blanc, I rouge," no fixed correspondence exists between sensations and vowels. Lilt reorchestrates both; context is all.

4. According to Dr. Lee Salk of the Cornell Medical Center, author of *What Every Child Wants His Parents to Know* (New York, Simon & Shuster, 1972), the tempo of both primitive and modern music is usually between 50 and 150 beats per minute, that of the heart, and babies already respond to such music in the first month. According to the Princeton Center for Infancy and Early Childhood, *The First Twelve Months of Life* (New York, Princeton, 1973), "Some doctors find that babies held in close contact with their mother's heart cry less. The heartbeat seems to soothe them, possibly because in the womb they have already heard their mother's heart."

5. Chiasmus (from the Greek for the cross-shaped letter X) is a common device of rhetoric but has not been previously used for X-ing start-of-line rhymes.

6. See Theodore Ziolkowski's summary of concentration camp writings in "The Literature of Atrocity," *Sewanee Review* (Winter 1977), p. 139.

7. Charles Tomlinson, *Poetry and Metamorphosis,* Cambridge University Press, London and New York, 1983, p. 71.

8. *Portrait of the Artist as an Old Dog:* Altered from Dylan Thomas's "Portrait of the Artist as a Young Dog," which in turn was altered from James Joyce's "Portrait of the Artist as a Young Man."

NOTE ON AUTHOR'S PREVIOUS BOOKS

Poetry: *New and Selected Poems,* 1967 (copies of first edition available only from author), and *The Persimmon Tree,* 1956, both out of print with the original publishers, are back in print since 1979 and 1965, respectively, with University Microfilms (300 North Zeeb Road, Ann Arbor, Mich. 48106, USA, and 18 Bedford Row, London WC1R 4EJ, England). Back in print since 1972–73 with Greenwood Press, 88 Post Road West, Westport, Conn. 06881, are *Terror and Decorum,* 1948; *Strike Through the Mask,* 1950; *The First Morning,* 1952; and *The Tree Witch,* 1961.

Prose: Since 1973 Greenwood Press has been reprinting *The Unadjusted Man: Reflections on the Distinction between Conserving and Conforming,* 1956, and since 1978 *Conservatism Revisited and the New Conservatism: What Went Wrong?,* 1949, 1965; *Shame and Glory of the Intellectuals: Babbitt Jr. versus the Rediscovery of Values,* 1953; *Conservatism from John Adams to Churchill: An Anthology and History,* 1956. Out of print: *Metapolitics: From the Romantics to Hitler,* N.Y., Knopf, 1941, and its revised updated paperback edition, *Metapolitics: The Roots of the Nazi Mind,* N.Y., Putnam Capricorn, 1961, 1965.

Glossary of Names, Foreign Phrases, Classical, Biblical, and Historical References *

Abelard. Medieval lover who was castrated.

Achtung. German for "attention": here used to mean the barking of authoritarian commands.

Ad astra per aspera. Latin motto meaning "to the stars through hardships."

Aedile (other earth). Town official in ancient Rome who supervised public works: hence, here blamed for Los Angeles smog in alternative universe.

Aegean. Arm of Mediterranean Sea between Asia Minor and Greece.

Agamemnon's carpet. Royal carpet welcoming Agamemnon home before he was treacherously murdered in his bath.

Aldebaran. The most brilliant of red stars; the Rumanian poet Tudor Arghezi has it representing a magical alternative universe.

Alexandrianizers. Stale epigones, as in the pedantry of Hellenistic Alexandria.

Anapest. Ta-ta-TUM.

Anno Domini and ano homini. Latin, respectively, for "in the year of our lord" and "in the anus of man."

Antaeus. In the Greek myth, Antaeus was the giant who gained strength by touching Mother Earth.

Aphrodite. Greek goddess of love.

Applewood. Here used as shorthand for the medieval legend that Christ's cross was made from the wood of Eden's appletree.

Aramaic. The Semitic language spoken by Christ.

---

*When "other earth" follows an item, it refers to the alternative universe of Cycle Three, where historical outcomes get reversed (e.g., see *Columbus*).

Arcadia, Arcady. Ancient Greek pastoral district; here used as metaphor for a garden of fruitful peace.

Aretê. Greek ideal of excellence.

Argonaut. In the Greek legend, Argonauts were adventurous mariners seeking the Golden Fleece.

Ariadne. Nietzsche's secret nickname (based on Cretan princess who gave Theseus thread for the labyrinth) for Wagner's wife Cosima, with whom he was obsessed.

Arnoldston, D.C. (other earth). In the alternative universe, it is the capital of America, named after Benedict Arnold, who was appointed British Governor of the defeated rebel colonies.

Attis (or Atys). Castrated son of Cybelê (worshipped by self-castrating priests in the Near East); together associated with spring resurrection.

Auschwitz. The most notorious of the Nazi death camps.

Baal. Baal is the supreme god of the ancient Canaanites for whom human sacrifices were burned alive.

Bacchus. Another name for Dionysus.

Bayreuth. Site of Wagner operas and festivals; here used as shorthand for romantic Wagnerian racist nationalism.

Boaz. Hebrew patriarch whose feet were warmed by young Ruth.

Bockelsen, Jan (a.k.a. John of Leiden, 1509–1536). Worshipped as dictator of the German town of Munster in 1533, he proclaimed himself king of the universe and proclaimed a social utopia of infinite love based on infinite terror, urging the slaughter of all aristocrats, Jews, the rich, and the clergy. In this book, this key figure keeps reappearing as ancestor of both Hitler and Lenin and represents that turning point where a well-meaning Christian love becomes secularized into the modern hate crusades of the totalitarian world "saviors."

Book one. Here used for Old Testament.

Book two. Here used for New Testament.

Borgia, Lucrezia (other earth). In the alternative universe, she is made the first woman pope for her piety and her wholesome cuisine.

Braunau. Austrian town where Hitler was born in 1889; here significant as same year Nietzsche went mad.

Bromio, Bromius. Names for Dionysus.

Brown, Norman O. (b. 1913). Twentieth-century crusader for "polymorph" sexual liberation.

Bryant, Anita (b. 1940). Twentieth-century crusader against sexual permissivenesss.

Calvary. From the Latin word "calvaria" for skull, it is the name for the hill near Jerusalem where Jesus was crucified (cf. *Golgotha*).

Cambrian period. Six hundred million years ago; part of the Paleozoic era; appearance of proto-eyed molluscs.

Capone, Al. The notorious Chicago gangster of the 1930s.

Carl. Churl or peasant; from "karl," Old Norse for "man."

Carnegie, Andrew (1835–1919). Nineteenth-century American captain of industry.

Ceres. Roman name for Greek harvest goddess, Demeter.

Certosa. Pious Carthusian monastery.

Chapmen. Old English for "tradesmen."

Charles the Anvil (other earth). In the alternative universe, he was defeated by Moslems in 732, making France an Arab-speaking nation. (In our own universe, Charles the Hammer won the battle.)

Charon. In the Greek myth, Charon is the ferryman of the dead to Hades; here he is identified with the nineteenth-century poet Thomas Lovell Beddoes.

Chutzpa. Yiddish for "brashness."

Circe. In the Greek legend, she turned men into swine, but here it is reversed to describe wives turning swine into men.

Columbus (other earth). In the alternative universe, the schlemiel who in 1492 fell off the edge of the earth because he mistakenly thought our flat world was round.

Cosima. Wife of Richard Wagner.

Credo quia absurdum. Latin for "I believe because it is absurd." [Usually attributed to the Carthaginian church father Tertullian (162?–230?) but garbled; his actual words were "Certum est quia impossibile est" (It is certain because it is impossible).]

Cronus. The Greek father god who devoured his children; sometimes identified (because of sound) with Greek "Chronos," meaning "Father Time."

Cybele. Phrygian goddess in one of the Hellenistic mystery religions competing with Christianity; likewise associated with spring resurrection; see *Attis.*

Cythera. Greek island where Aphrodite was born from the sea.

Dactyl. TUM-ta-ta.

Dagon. Fish god of the ancient Philistines.

Daw, Marjorie. The seesawing young lady of the Mother Goose jingle.

Demeter. See *Ceres.*

De Mille, Cecil B. (1881–1959). Director of movie spectaculars; here cited for his crucifixion film.

Dionysus. Green wine god whose vine limbs were annually hacked and re-sprouted in a pre-Christian version of the Easter resurrection (also known as Bacchus, Bromio, and Zagreus); here representing the long-lost pagan half of the returning Son of Man.

DNA. Acronym for deoxyribonucleic acid. Refers to the strands of living cell nuclei, twisted into a "double helix," which carry out the instructions of the genes controlling heredity.

Dordogne. Here used as shorthand for the caves painted by prehistoric man (cf. Lascaux).

Ecce homo. Latin for "behold the man," Pontius Pilate's reference to Christ; also the title of Nietzsche's autobiographical notes when he was going mad and signing himself Christ-Dionysus, 1888–1889.

Ecce homunculus. In medieval magic, a homunculus was a tiny human figure, a mannikin produced by sorcerers, here used to parody "ecce homo."

Edwards, Jonathan (1703–1758). American theologian who preached in North-ampton, Massachusetts. Here used in connection with "tiger" metaphor for God because one of his bloodcurdling sermons compared God to a raging tiger confronting sinners.

Eichmann, Adolf (1906–1962). Nazi official who rounded up Jews for the "final solution."

Eohippus. The primeval rabbit-size ancestor of the horse.

Erg. Unit for measuring energy.

Eros-Thanatos. Greek for the double deity "Love-Death."

Eumenides. Greek euphemism for the Furies.

Fjeld. High, barren Scandinavian plateau; from Old Norse.

Foamborn. Sea-born Aphrodite.

Forum. Central square of ancient Rome.

Francis. Saint Francis is here referred to as taming savage animals through love.

Galilee, Galilean. Reference to Christ, who came from ancient Galilee (cf. *Julian the Apostate*).

Ganges. Here this sacred river is used as the would-be sanctification of all bodily exudings.

Geo. From Ge, the Greek earth goddess; hence, "geometry," here used as trying in vain to measure this immeasurable deity.

Gibbon, Edward (1737–1794). Author of a classic history of imperial downfall (here used in analogy with American parallels), *The Decline and Fall of the Roman Empire.* Hence, in Cycle Three, the "Tiber matron" (Rome personified) first "declines" the advances of the barbarian invader, then "falls" for him.

Ghaut (Ghat). Funeral pyre where widows of Hindu princes were burned; here used for the reddening of leaves in autumn.

Golgotha. Aramaic for skull is "gogoltha," Hebrew "gulgoleth." In Matthew 27:33, this is the Place of Skulls (Calvary hill) near Jerusalem where Jesus was crucified (cf. *Calvary*).

Goths. Invading Germanic tribe that helped destroy the Roman empire.

Götterdämmerung. Twilight of the (Germanic) gods; also title of Wagner opera.

Götzendämmerung. German for "twilight of the idols," coined by Nietzsche to parody Wagner's Götterdämmerung, q.v.

Hades. The Greek hell; underground kingdom of Pluto.

Hagen. Murderous leader in the medieval German Nibelung epic, circa 1200. Here mentioned to characterize the Germany of World War II (more desperate and more lone-wolfish than Siegfried who was the German hero of World War I). Like Hitler, Hagen fought to the end in an underground bunker, exhorting his Germanic followers to "tread down the flames in blood."

Hagenkreuz. Here used as an amalgam coinage to combine Hagen (q.v.) with Hakenkreuz (q.v.).

Hakenkreuz. German word for "swastika," the official Nazi emblem.

Helicon. Mountain of the Muses in Greece, near Gulf of Corinth.

Hellenic. Greek civilization, here contrasted both with Christianity and with the corruption of Hellenic into Hellenistic, q.v. Greece was called Hellas from the seventh century B.C. on.

Hellenistic. The diluted form of Hellenic culture diffused in Asia and later in the Roman empire after Alexander the Great, and into the first century A.D. Here used as a sugary, superstitious, less genuine Hellenism. One aspect of the Hellenistic culture was its mystery religions, i.e., the "born again" messianic mass religions of the first century A.D., including Mithraism, cults of Cybelê and Isis, and Christianity.

Helios. Greek sun god.

Humani nihil a me alienum puto. Latin for "I deem nothing human alien to me"; from a play by Terence (c. 190–159 B.C.)

Hygeia. Health goddess.

Hypocrite lecteur. A famous phrase from the poet Charles Baudelaire, meaning "hypocritical reader."

Iambic. Ta-TUM.

Ignis fatuus. Medieval Latin for "foolish fire"; here the misleading marshfire on Land's End.

In hoc signo. From the quotation "in hoc signo vinces," Latin for "in this sign thou shalt conquer," here used as code language for the change of Christianity from underground religion to imperial power state; inspired by this motto in a dream, the Roman emperor Constantine (272–337) defeated his opponents and made Christianity the state religion.

INRI. Latin acronym for Jesus of Nazareth, king of the Jews; used mockingly by his crucifiers.

Isis. Egyptian love goddess who gathered the scattered pieces of Osiris and in some versions straddled his erect corpse in order to give birth to the sun again after winter.

Jackboots. Part of the Nazi storm-troop apparel.

Jacta est alea. Latin for "the die is cast"; Julius Caesar's remark in 49 B.C. on crossing the Rubicon; here used to mean taking the risk of a decisive gamble.

Jarl. Ancient Scandinavian nobleman (earl).

Jones, Reverend Jim. A recent American cult leader who killed his fanatic followers with poisoned Kool-Aid.

Jones, Maggie. Here Mary Magdalen is given a common name to represent a modern Aphrodite.

Judenstern. German for "Jewish star," a yellow badge Jews were forced to wear in Nazi Germany.

Julian the Apostate (331?–363). The fourth-century Roman emperor who, vainly trying to halt the triumph of Christianity, allegedly said, "vicisti Galilaee," Latin for "thou hast conquered, O Galilean."

Khan, Genghis (1167?–1227). Founder of Mongol empire; here typifying omnipotent ruthlessness.

Kulturbolshevizing. Criticism of German culture was denounced by Nazis with this German term for "cultural bolshevism."

Lacrimae rerum. Latin for "the tears of things," from the *Aeneid* of Virgil, 70–19 B.C.

Lady Greensleeves. Character in British ballad; here used to represent growth and fertility.

Lamb. Christ as a sacrificial animal.

Lascaux. The painted Cro-Magnon caves in Dordogne, an area in southern France.

Lessing, Gotthold Ephraim (1729–1781). Eighteenth-century German author whose play "Nathan the Wise" argued for a tolerant attitude toward Jews; here used in connection with Wagner's bloodthirsty joke that all Jews should be invited to see a performance of "Nathan" and then be locked in and burnt alive.

Lethe. In Greek legend, it is the name of the stream of the dead bringing forgetfulness by washing away memory.

Limēs. Latin for the "border" of the Roman empire.

Loamborn. Eve as earth mother.

Loo. British slang for latrine.

Lot's wife. In Old Testament, Lot's wife, was turned to salt as punishment for looking back on the destruction of Sodom and Gomorrah.

Luddites. Smashers of machinery in early nineteenth-century England.

Lungfish. The first air-breathing fish.

Mankine (sic). Mankind renamed as cattle in father's slaughterhouse.

Manson, Charles. The "mystical" mass murderer of California cultism; note that "Manson" is a reversal of "Son [of] Man."

Märchen. German word for "fairy tale."

Marx, Groucho (b. 1895). Movie actor known for sardonic humor.

Mary. Older Mary refers to mother of Jesus; younger or "other" Mary refers to Mary Magdalen.

Meshuga. Yiddish word for "nutty."

Metics. In ancient Greek cities, the metics were usually foreign-merchant residents, lacking regular citizenship and discriminated against by xenophobes. In modern France, anti-Dreyfusards sometimes denounced French Jews as "metics."

Milquetoast. Cartoon character known as the "timid soul."

Milt. Semen.

Mimosa. A plant so sensitive it seems to wince when touched.

Mithra. Hellenistic god popular among Roman soldiers; of Persian origin; his religion was a serious competitor with early Christianity.

Mors vincit omnia. Latin phrase for "death conquers all"; here coined as reversal of the cliché "amor vincit alia" ("love conquers all").

Muses. Nine goddesses presiding over the various arts. When used in singular, "Muse" refers to Euterpe, the muse of lyric poetry and music.

Nietzsche, Friedrich (1844–1900). The German philosopher who, breaking with Richard Wagner, was the first to warn that Wagnerian anti-Semitism would lead to a Jewish "bloodbath." In view of the later misuse of Nietzsche by German nationalists, note his prophetic foreboding of 1885 in the preface to his unfinished book, *The Will to Power:* ". . . a book for *thinking,* nothing else. . . . That it is written in German is untimely to say the least: I wish I had written it in French so that it might not appear to be a confirmation of the aspirations of the German Reich."

Nietzsche went mad in 1889 (perhaps of syphilis, perhaps not) and died in 1900. Torn between several generations of Lutheran-minister ancestry and his quixotic aim to become "the Anti-Christ" and to worship Dionysus, Nietzsche is here treated as half-brother—in his via dolorosa—of the Son of Man. Most cycles begin with an epigraph from Nietzsche.

Niobe. Weeping Niobe was the Greek archetype of motherly love. All fourteen of her children were slain by the gods; though changed into stone, she kept on weeping.

Nomen omen. Latin for "name as omen" (cf. *Hagenkreuz*).

Norns. Nordic version of the three fates spinning the threads of human lives.

Noyades (les). From the French meaning "the drownings." In 1794, Jean Baptiste Carrier (call him a John the Baptist of modern Procrustean ideologues) sentenced thousands of alleged counterrevolutionaries in France to "Republican marriages"; that is, naked males and females were bound face to face and drowned in the Loire.

Obol. Greek coin; the fee paid to ferryman Charon, q.v.

Olympus. Mountain in Thessaly where the Greek gods resided.

O Mensch! Gib Acht! This quotation from a poem by Nietzsche means: "O man, pay heed."

Onan. Condemned in Old Testament (Genesis 38:9) for "spilling his seed." Onanism today means masturbation.

Oom. Here used to mean the continuous pendulum between womb and tomb.

Orpheus. In the Greek myth, Orpheus descended to the kingdom of death (Hades) to look for his beloved.

Osiris. Egyptian god cut into fourteen pieces each winter but reborn in spring; sometimes associated with Dionysus legend.

Our Lady Diamat (other earth). Memo from future universe of 2500: 'The name of Our Lady Diamat of Holy Russia is derived from that mysterious archaism of 1917, "dia-lectical mat-erialism," its meaning lost over the centuries. We ingenious linguists of 2500 have deduced from Latin the two halves composing the word "Diamat": "Dia" for goddess, "mat" for "mater" or mother, hence "mater-ism"— an ism expressing the Slavic soul's cult of Our Lady's motherly spirituality.'

Pagliacci. Tragic clown in Italian opera; here one aspect of Nietzsche.

Paleozoic. Geologic era, from 600 million to 280 million years ago; Devonian period, circa 405 million years ago, part of the Paleozoic era; first appearance of lungfish and amphibians.

Pan. Greek nature god, shaggy and goatfooted. Son of Man returns to try to merge with Dionysus (also sometimes represented as goat) and Pan.

Pandora. In the Greek myth, by opening a forbidden box, Pandora released terrifying surprises.

Papa Doc (Francois Duvalier, 1907–1971). This nickname of the Haitian despot is here used as shorthand for enshrined, arbitrary tyranny.

Parnassus. Hill sacred to Apollo and the Muses in central Greece.

Paul. St. Paul of Tarsus (died c. 67 A.D.) is here seen as falsifier—that is, ideologizer and propagandist—of Christ's teachings, making them a bureaucracy of power. "The man who, I suppose, did more than anybody else to distort and subvert Christ's teaching was Paul. . . . It would be hard to imagine anything more un-Christlike than Christian theology."—From the *Dialogues of Alfred North Whitehead.*

Pavlov, Ivan (1849–1936). Russian scientist who experimented with the conditioned reflexes of salivating dogs.

Peale, Norman Vincent (b. 1898). Twentieth-century crusader for optimistic middle-class proprieties.

Peccavi (Walter) pater. An amalgam of the Latin confession "peccavi, pater" meaning "I have sinned, father" and that philosopher of aestheticism, Walter Pater (1839–1894).

Pentheus. Theban ruler destroyed by Dionysus.

Persephone. Greek goddess, daughter of Demeter-Ceres. She was condemned to spend the wintry half of the year underground with Pluto in Hades, but arose—with the resprouting flowers—every spring; sometimes associated with the similarly resprouting Dionysus.

Peter. In the Gospel of Saint Matthew, 16:18, Christ said to Saint Peter: "And I say also unto thee, that thou art Peter, and upon this rock I will build my church." Since Saint Peter was the first Bishop of Rome, Christ's wordplay on "petra" (Greek for rock) and "Petros" (Greek for Peter) is often interpreted as the foundation stone of the Roman Catholic church.

Phaëthon. In the Greek myth, Phaëthon was killed when driving the flaming chariot of his father, the sun god Helios.

Phoenix. In the Greek myth, the bird, Phoenix, was reborn in the flames of its own funeral pyre.

Piero della Francesca (1420–1492). Italian painter; here mentioned because his Resurrection portrait gives Christ the hauntingly bleak eyes of someone who has been three days underground.

Pilate, Pontius. Roman procurator of Judaea during c. 26–c. 36 A.D. when Jesus was crucified; see *ecce homo.*

Plainte éternelle. French phrase meaning "eternal lament."

Pleistocene period. Six hundred thousand years ago; appearance of modern man and many large mammals.

Pluto. The name's Greek meaning, "wealth giver," means the harborer of the buried winter seed, but this positive side is far outweighed by the god's negative role as representing the annual death of vegetation. Pluto is king of Hades, the underground of the dead.

Poseidon. Greek god of ocean.

Primavera. Italian word for "spring."

Procrustes. Greek bandit who fatally lopped off or stretched his victim's limbs to fit his bed; here used as representing rigid ideologizing.

Prometheus. The Titan who stole fire (here used for sexual fire) from heaven and gave it to man. Zeus punished him by chaining him to a rock; in this case, to a latrine.

Proserpine. Roman name for Greek goddess Persephone, q.v.

Prospero. Master of the barbarous Caliban in Shakespeare's *Tempest;* here used to personify an often-misguided scientific progress.

Proteus. Greek shape-changing god, here representing pluralist adaptability.

Reich, Wilhelm (1897–1957). Twentieth-century Austrian psychiatrist and crusader for sexual liberation.

Romany. Gypsy as well as gypsy language; here used to represent exotic glamor.

Santa Kitsch. An amalgam of Santa Claus, a sentimental Germanic heritage, and "kitsch," German word for a soupy banality.

Sargasso. Far, warm, seaweed-covered sea where eels reputedly go to breed.

Schicklgruber. Original surname of Hitler's father. Had son Adolf retained the name, "Heil Schicklgruber" would have lacked the charisma of "Heil Hitler."

Schliemann, Heinrich (1822–1890). From the text, "Schliemann mole" is a reference to the German archeologist digging nine cities deep in search of ancient Troy.

Sieg Heil. Nazi salutation.

Siegfried. Germanic hero of Wagnerian opera and also of German nationalism in World War I.

Sir Benedict: See *Arnoldston, D.C. (other earth).*

Sistine Chapel face. Here used for the stern patriarchal forehead and eyes painted by Michelangelo (1475–1564) on the roof of the Sistine Chapel in Rome.

Skald. Ancient Scandinavian bard.

Skull Hill. The hill of Golgotha near Jerusalem.

Son of Man. The New Testament reference to Christ in his human incarnation.

Spondee. TUM-TUM (accent on both syllables).

Stabat Mater. Latin for "the mother was standing," taken from church music about Mary's suffering while standing at the crucifixion of her son.

Styx. River across which the dead were ferried by Charon.

Swanboat. A prop of Wagner's Lohengrin opera.

Tarsus. A partly Romanized, partly Hellenistic town in Asia Minor, home of Saint Paul.

Thane. A Scandinavian lord, higher than a freeman but lower than a nobleman.

Thomas. Saint Thomas was Christ's doubting disciple; here used as Peeping Saint Thomas, an amalgam with Peeping Tom (a voyeur).

Tiber. Rome's river.

Timburlane. Mongol ruler known for his cruelty; here also a reference to his Samarkand tomb of black onyx.

Trochee. TUM-ta.

Trotskigrad (other earth). In the alternative universe, it is the capital of Russia after Trotsky's successful exposure of Stalin as a secret member of the tsarist police. "Grad" is Russian for "city."

Tyrannosaurus rex. Latin for "tyrant-lizard king," the largest of the extinct dinosaurs.

Vanitas vanitatum. Latin for "vanity of vanities." Ecclesiastes in the Old Testament is here rebuked for denouncing the alleged "vanity" of all this-worldly human concerns.

Venus. Roman name for the Greek Aphrodite.

Venusberg. Aphrodite-Venus, no longer above ground as in the classical era, was driven underground by Christianity (parallel with the repressed "subconscious" mind) into Venusberg.

Via dolorosa. Stages of the Cross in Christ's climb up Golgotha.